How to Sell Technology

How to Sell Technology®

"Hunt Now, or Be Eaten Later!®"

The Value Forward Method

PAUL DiMODICA

Johnson-Hunter, Inc. Peachtree City, Georgia 30269

First edition published 2000. Seventh edition published 2012.

Printed in the United States of America

ISBN-13: 978-1-933598-55-0

Table of Contents

Preface

Welcome, Technology Sales Professional! Thank you for investing in my IT sales training course.

Since this book's first publication in 2001, I have received thousands of emails and letters from around the world—from IT salespeople, sales managers, vice presidents of sales, and CEOs of both public and private technology, software, and professional service companies—thanking me for this body of work and its contents.

I have heard from salespeople who have aggressively surpassed their assigned IT sales quotas, from technology firms that have doubled their revenues, and from vice presidents of sales whose entire teams have gone from failure to success following the methods in this book, all in less than one year.

In this updated version, we have added more strategies, tactics, and methodologies based on what works in today's economy, coupled with more IT case studies to help you build a replicable and scalable sales process that will increase your speed to success.

My name is Paul DiModica. I am the CEO and founder of the Value Forward Group (www.ValueForward.com). The Value Forward Group is a high tech business success advisement firm. At the Value Forward Group, we also publish *High Tech Success* (www.HighTechSuccess.com), our best practices newsletter. *High Tech Success* is the world's largest IT business success newsletter. It focuses on technology sales, marketing, and strategy best practices, and is read worldwide.

At the Value Forward Group, we specialize in advising CEOs and senior management teams of technology, software, and professional service companies, from start-up to Global 1000 companies, on success best practices. The Value Forward Group uses a holistic revenue capture process where we integrate sales, marketing, strategy, finance, and operations into one outbound IT revenue capture method.

Since 2001, we have worked with more than 600 CEOs of IT companies on best practices growth of which more than 50 were global IT companies.

During my career as an IT salesperson, I have competed against high-priced consulting firms, low-cost providers, regional players, aggressive venture capital funded start-ups, Fortune 100 sales organizations, and hardware and software companies that are dominant in their vertical spaces. But it doesn't matter. I believe that **selling technology and professional services is a premeditated sport**. With best practice knowledge, a precise roadmap, and consistent practice, you can prepare for the big game, and on any given Sunday, more times than not, you can beat anybody.

My original sales process was called the Rhino IT Sales method. Today, it has morphed into the Value Forward Revenue Capture program.

Using the *Value Forward Revenue Capture* method, professional salespeople (and the marketing, strategy, operations, and executive teams) focus on using a premeditated sales approach that integrates marketing, strategy, sales process, and financial management into one outbound revenue capture program. The program trains technology salespeople *how to become a peer in the boardroom, instead of a vendor waiting in the hallway*.

Simple concept, but important message.

Based on the Value Forward program, I put into play a long and successful career as a corporate technology major sales account manager, a vice president of sales and marketing, and a company founder. The *Value Forward Sales* method works, selling business owners of privately held businesses that do $10 million a year as well as CEOs, CFOs, and CIOs of Global 1000 firms.

Using premeditated sales as my guiding principle, I developed the *Value Forward Sales* method through personal experiences, detailed research, clients' experiences, experiential education, and trial and error to help other technology salespeople and growth directed management teams like you sell more, eliminate competition, and increase their sales dramatically.

It doesn't matter if your business is a one-person IT start-up or a global company. If you sell technology professional services, enterprise applications, web application development, SaaS (software as a service), shrink-wrapped software applications, managed services, electronic or hardware equipment, or consulting on a daily basis, you are faced with an increasing stable of competitors and barriers to sales that frustrate you as a quota-carrying technology major account manager or a small IT shop trying to make payroll. Even worse, if you are a technology sales vice president managing a direct sales force, the number of salespeople you are responsible for multiplies your frustration.

Having been an IT salesperson like you, I understand your frustration. I was constantly exposed to market walls that tried to prevent me from meeting my sales quotas. Through this program, you will learn how to sell technology services and applications of all types quickly, efficiently, and profitably, in spite of the business impediments that stand in your way. My sales training program has worked with small technology start-ups as well as mature, established companies. In a world where competition erodes market share and depresses service and software pricing, and where branding and marketing trample the start-up or small business owner, the key is not *first* to market—the key is *smart* to market.

To be honest, I have spent a dominant amount of my IT sales and sales management career working with firms that were aggressively pursuing markets that were very competitive. The "David versus Goliath" scenario was a constant reality for me. So, I always had to work smarter rather than harder. Some firms I worked with were venture capital launch companies with minimal revenue, entrenched competitors, and no clear market differentiation. Others were mature players with little funding for new research and development. No matter what kind of technology services, software, or applications you sell, by the time you finish reading about the *Value Forward Sales* method, you will have obtained the knowledge you need to become more productive and to increase your income, your wealth, and your career success.

As you go through this program, I recommend that you highlight areas that are important to you. Once completed, go through the course again and put together a Marketing Action Plan (M.A.P.—more on this later in the book) to implement your new attack on technology sales.

So, let's get going. Sit back, get comfortable, and let's rumble through the selling technology jungle.

In IT, it's "Hunt Now, or Be Eaten Later!®"

Sincerely,

Paul R. DiModica
Value Forward Group
pdimodica@valueforward.com
770-632-7647

How to Use This Book

Everyone lives by selling something. –Robert Louis Stevenson

This book is designed to be a useful business tool for IT salespeople, vice presidents of sales, and high tech CEOs looking to increase their current sales capture program success. Although set up in a book format, the material is laid out as a training course to help you walk through your sales process.

I am sure you have read lots of sales books, most filled with theories, strategies, and under-described sales techniques that don't fully explain what you as a salesperson should do to increase your success.

That is not this book.

This book is written from an instructional point of view, with case studies to help you build an action step plan of what you need to say, present, and implement immediately to sell more technology, software, and professional services. In fact, my firm has taught these techniques live to tens of thousands of IT salespeople worldwide. We have trained individual players, mature family-run IT companies, venture capital funded players, and Global 50 company major account sales teams.

Through this publication we are going to teach you:

- How to communicate value to management

- How to talk peer to peer

- How to generate qualified IT leads

- How to penetrate the no talk zone of management

- How to set up your first meeting with management

- How to determine if prospects are qualified buyers or professional lookers

- How to do executive briefings and webinars that induce management prospects to take action steps to buy

- How to sell more, work less, and increase your IT sales income dramatically

Study this book. With effort and practice, it will help you become the most successful and highest paid IT salesperson in your company.

Let the games begin!

Technology Sales Is a Premeditated Sport.

Selling technology in our current market space is based on survival:

- Survival of the best-equipped salesperson

- Survival of the salesperson who works the hardest

- Survival of the salesperson who wants to win

- Survival of the IT salesperson who has ambition

  The price of success is hard work, dedication to the job at hand, and the determination that whether we win or lose, we have applied the best of ourselves to the task at hand. –Vince Lombardi

I can teach you how to find clients, how to present like a pro, and how to close contracts, but I cannot teach you the desire to succeed. If you can't pick up the phone and cold call, or answer the proposal objections from a tough CEO of a large company, or handle the drilling and probing of a small business owner—all because you are afraid—then you should get out of technology sales.

Yes—you should quit being an IT salesperson. During the dot com days, lots of history, political science, or computer engineering majors fell into technology sales and stayed there because the money was easy, the job was independent, and stock options were plenty.

Not anymore.

IT sales is a tough business. Are you tough enough? Do you have ambition, or are you just hanging on, hoping to sell some "gravy" key account that will pay your way until you move on to your next job?

If you don't have ambition, if you are not prepared to practice your craft, then IT sales—professional IT sales—is not for you.

Selling technology is a contact sport. If you have been selling for longer than one year, you have been bruised. Yet, if you sell correctly, you can escape the pain and maximize your success.

Hunters own the jungle!

Chapter

1

Who Are You? Why Should Prospects Buy From You?

After reading this section, you will learn:

- How the *Value Forward Sales* method is different

- How to develop a unique Sales Value Proposition

- How to paint a picture that makes executives listen

History of the *Value Forward Sales* Method and Why You Should Use Our Approach

You may be wondering: Where did the *Value Forward Sales* method come from?

In 1984, after serving four years in the U.S. Navy, I left the service with an undergraduate degree in business administration and part of my MBA completed. I took an IT sales position in Boston, Massachusetts, with a venture capital funded high tech company based in Toronto, Canada, a company called Remanco Systems.

As I started my IT sales career, I was full of hope and anticipation of achieving great personal satisfaction from doing a job well done and earning a large income. This Canadian company had hired me to sell point-of-sales (POS) systems to restaurants and hotels. The position required me to sell POS systems that included software, hardware, cabling, training, and maintenance contracts as one integrated solution to independent restaurant owners in Boston.

The term POS was new to me and to most restaurant prospects in 1984. In fact, the more common term (although not technically a correct description for what we sold) was "cash registers."

Our POS system was state-of-the-art technology and had technical superiority over anything available in the market at that time. It allowed restaurant employees to take customers' orders from the dining room and send them to printers in the kitchen with specific cooking instructions. Once the customers completed their meals, our system calculated tax, tips, and separate billings for each customer at a table and then allowed the wait staff to "settle" the bill at the table through a unique process called "cashier banking." Cashier banking is where the wait staffers collect all the money and credit card charges for their table assignments during their shifts, and then at the end of the day, they close out their billings with the POS system (and the manager's approval).

These unique features eliminated the need for a cashier and expensive bar-coded printed checks, and the POS system increased the number of customers served on a shift (through more table turns), which increased the restaurant's total daily revenue.

Above and beyond the great features and functions of our software was our POS system's actual technical design. The system was a true central processing unit POS that operated on an Intel 8086 chip and eight-inch floppy discs, and it ran on Digital Research's CPM operating system. This was cutting-edge technology. Our system allowed us to operate up to 25 dumb POS terminals simultaneously without any speed or transaction problems. Pretty amazing for 1984!

So, how was our firm going to grow its corporate revenues? And more important to me, how was I going to make my annual IT sales quota ($1 million in 1984 dollars), pay my mortgage, and keep my job?

During my first few weeks with Remanco, I received one week of sales training, one week of product training, and did a ride along with a sales manager for some prospect demos. I was told that if I was successful after the first year, I would be transferred to Hartford, Connecticut and promoted to a regional sales manager position.

After I had been with the company for 60 days with zero sales, my boss Steve came to me and said, "Paul, I want you to move Hartford and open up a new office."

Surprised by the early request, I asked, "With a promotion?"

Steve retorted, "Hell, no—you haven't sold anything yet!"

So off I went, relocating to an undersized, ugly condo with four doors and three windows in a small town outside of

Hartford. In Connecticut, my dream of IT sales success continued to elude me.

Several problems contributed to my lack of success. My high tech management team forgot to mention a few things to me (conveniently) during my pre-employment sales interview, including:

1. Most restaurant owners in 1984 were afraid of computers and software.

2. Restaurant owners hated too much technology because they liked the cash availability of their business and too much automation created an audit trail for the U.S. Internal Revenue Service to follow.

3. National Cash Register (NCR), a Fortune 500 company, had invented the cash register and had over 80 percent market share penetration in the restaurant industry in 1984.

4. My POS system cost 100 percent more than NCR's system on an average proposal.

Let me repeat the last point. **My technology system's price was 100 percent more money than the system from the Fortune 500 company that had created the market and currently had 80 percent market share.**

Like most new IT salespeople, I struggled day in and day out during my first weeks of employment, trying to figure out what I needed to do to hit my sales quota. After much thought and frustration, I came up with three basic questions that I, as an IT salesperson, needed to answer:

- Why should my prospects buy from me?

- Why would my prospects not buy from me?
- How do I create value for my prospects that they will believe?

Simple questions—but when I asked my local management team and our corporate marketing vice president in Canada for some intellectual support on these issues, all I got were PR platitudes that never seemed to induce prospects to take an action step to buy. All I heard was "Tell them we have the best computer system," or "We have the best support," or "They can save money on their costs of restaurant operations."

This was all management gobbledygook, nonproductive corporate speak that made the communicators seem out of touch with what it took to sell in a competitive marketplace to buyers who were technically afraid of a system that was 100 percent more money than the system from the Fortune 500 industry founder that had 80 percent of the market share.

Great Stuff! Unbelievable Technology, But No Sales

At a meeting at corporate headquarters in Toronto, with all the sales and marketing team members present, my CEO gave us a leadership pep talk about how superior our technology was and how we were going to be the next IBM of the restaurant industry! Great, I thought, but tell me how to sell this IT system, how marketing is going to generate qualified leads for me, and better yet—tell me why my prospects should buy from us instead of NCR, the dominant market share leader. Also, tell me how to keep my job, hit my assigned sales quota, and make some money!

A lot of expectations from a young buck IT salesperson!

After 11 weeks of no sales, no proposal negotiations, and boxes of free marketing collateral the company had instructed me to hand out, I decided to take some time off from my job (before I was fired) and think through the three questions that continued to trouble me.

During my sales sabbatical, I read a book about entrepreneurship called *Advanced Rhinocerology* by Scott Alexander.

It's a little book about being an entrepreneur and becoming successful. It's filled with lots of pictures and big ideas. In *Rhinocerology*, Alexander talks about two types of people in the world: Cows and Rhinos. According to Alexander, Cows weigh 2,000 pounds, have small brains, eat the grass they stand on, and are afraid of lighting. Rhinos also weigh 2,000 pounds, but the similarities end there. Rhinos have two-inch-thick skin and two-foot-long horns, they rumble through the jungle, and they are afraid of nothing. In his book, Alexander compares people to Cows and Rhinos. Sometimes people are afraid of everything, and sometimes they take on the world without fear.

During the first couple days of my self-imposed vacation, I must admit I acted like a Cow, whining "Poor is me; no one will buy my technology." But after two days of mooing, I finally regained hold of my senses and decided to act like a Rhino. It was time to take some action steps on my own.

To help me understand why I was failing, I went back to my original POS prospects, the ones who were not interested in what I had to offer. I talked to restaurant owners about their operational business problems, their personal needs as self-employed entrepreneurs, and why (or why not) they would spend money on technology. I wanted to identify why they would spend $80,000.00 on a walk-in freezer or why they had someone build a Brazilian mahogany bar on premise for them for $150,000.00, but they would not buy a technically superior POS system from me.

Once I heard their responses, I sat down and created from scratch my own IT sales and marketing methodology—out of fear of losing my job—to help me sell more so I could pay the mortgage on my house I had left behind in Boston. Using this self-developed technology sales and marketing approach, I went on to sell over $1.3 million (in 1984 dollars) of software, hardware, training, and maintenance contracts the first year, and I ended up getting promoted twice during my first 12 months of employment.

As my career advanced, I was promoted to senior vice president of sales and marketing, vice president of operations/engineering, and vice president of strategy in several different technology, software, and professional service companies with annual revenues up to $1 billion. I also started two IT companies. As my career evolved, I expanded the *Value Forward Sales* method, now part of the *Value Forward High Tech Success System*, to include strategy, financial management, operations, and development, and I have used my system in every firm I have worked in, started, or advised.

Why Most Technology Sales Training Methods Fail

Since 2001, I have advised hundreds of IT CEOs of privately held technology, software, and professional service companies and 50 of the largest global IT firms on best practice growth strategies. Our firm focuses on a holistic revenue capture process, where we integrate sales, marketing, strategy, operations, and financial management departments into one outbound revenue capture program.

As a high tech business success advisement firm, we work holistically across the board with all departments to help them maximize their business efficiencies and strategies based on a studied best practices approach. But the one department that seems to need the most help on a recurring basis is the sales department.

As an IT salesperson, you know that sales success is a company responsibility, not just the onus of the sales team. Yet, day in and day out, you are blamed when you miss your sales quota or when an important deal is lost.

But is it really your fault?

Yes ... and no!

No, because if your software or service offerings are buggy, your support is terrible, your operations vice president can't get the new app releases out the door, your CEO is taking all the company's research and development money out of your privately held company to buy a new yacht on the Potomac, or you are trying to sell blue shoes to a red shoe market—then lack of success does not fall on your shoulders.

Yes, because it's your sales quota, and if you are a professional IT salesperson, ultimately you need to be successful in spite of the business environment and company limitations under which you operate. You can always blame your company—and often it might be your company's fault—but aren't *you* supposed to be a sales *professional*?

Over and above operating in the wrong sales environment, the primary reason most IT salespeople fail today is because they use the wrong sales process. I know, you have read all the integrity, spin, questioning, and strategic solution sales books on how to sell.

So, how is your IT sales success going?

If not so good, here's why. Unlike the success method I offer, those other methods were not developed from the ground up for IT sales. Instead, the book authors tried to adapt their methods to the technology market. Even worse, their methods misrepresent and direct IT salespeople through a complicated selling process where hope becomes a sales forecast.

All those other methods sound great. They appeal to IT salespeople's needs to be liked and to create a mutually satisfying selling-buying process where all prospects are honorable, sincere, honest, and never misleading.

But that's not how it works. Hey, this isn't the Boy Scouts!

This is the real world.

Selling IT software and professional services is a unique process. It's not the same as selling financial services, waste management, stocks and bonds, wholesale supplies, or jet engines.

Selling IT calls for a unique process of time management.

Are your current IT sales up in this economy?

Are you hitting or exceeding your IT sales quota?

Are you happy with the current sales process your company developed or you gleaned from a book?

If so, then stop; don't read any further because you're wasting your valuable time reading my book. Go make as much money as possible using those other methods.

But if you are *not* blowing away your IT sales quota, or if your sales team or IT company is not growing revenues at an accelerated rate using a replicable and scalable sales process, or if you individually as an IT salesperson are not getting rich—then this book is for you.

One warning, though! The *Value Forward Sales* method takes effort, practice, premeditation of action steps, and ambition. My method is not for everyone. It's for IT salespeople who are professionals. One reason some IT salespeople are not successful using my approach is that they do not put in the effort required to be successful. Why? Because they are lazy.

They are always looking for the easy way to get rich.

Or they want their management team to feed them cherry accounts or prequalified leads so they can just take orders.

That's not selling.

Instead, these unsuccessful salespeople revert to marketing IT and professional services the way they have always sold—based on relationships, being subservient to prospects, and making it more complex than it should be.

The *Value Forward Sales* method is the thinking IT salesperson's program.

All the other sales methods just confuse and complicate the straightforward business of selling technology and services. Their approaches to sales actually create an artificial success perception for IT salespeople who follow their recommendations to the letter—and still fail.

Why?

Because these methods elongate the IT sales process, filling sales pipelines with deals that don't get closed, forcing salespeople to misread IT professional lookers as IT buyers, and turning off management prospects ... who then don't buy.

Selling IT is a premeditated sport. It is a thinking process based on specific action steps, managed in a sequential process by the seller, prodding the buyer in tandem.

If you study our approaches, implement our tactics and techniques, and apply our communication process, you can become the top IT salesperson in your company. You will find yourself selling IT to CEOs of small, privately held companies as well as to C-level executives in multiple-step process deals in Global 1000 firms.

If you have attended any of our company sales training programs, public sales and sales management events, or CEO How to Grow Your IT Business seminars, have read my newsletter, or have been coached individually by us, you know our approach challenges the status quo on how most IT sales teams sell and how most technology firms capture revenue.

If this is your first exposure to our processes and methodologies, I guarantee you will have to rethink and re-educate yourself on the basic approaches you use to present and sell technology and services.

If you believe you are a senior salesperson, let me challenge you to have an open mind about what that really means.

Often, IT salespeople describe themselves as senior salespeople based on the years of experience they have. But time in employment is not a criterion for senior success measurement. Senior IT salespeople are those candidates who can find, manage, and close qualified prospects by themselves during a short time frame, regardless of the operating environment and conditions their company places on them and regardless of the size of their IT offering's price point or the complexity of the technology they sell.

So, even if you are an experienced IT salesperson—try our approach. Our methods work. We will teach you how to become a peer in the boardroom who sells more, instead of a vendor waiting in the hallway hoping for a sale. If you will keep an open mind, you can increase your IT sales success … starting immediately.

In IT sales, you have a choice. Act like a vendor … or act like a peer. Act like a Cow … or act like a Rhino … and sell more.

It's up to you.

*Your time is limited, so don't waste it living
someone else's life. Don't be trapped by
dogma—which is living with the results of
other people's thinking. Don't let the noise of
others' opinions drown out your own inner
voice. And most important, have the courage
to follow your heart and intuition. They
somehow already know what you truly want to
become. Everything else is secondary.*

–Steve Jobs

The Five Fallacies of Technology Sales

Selling technology, software, and professional service
methods is full of fallacies manufactured by sales coaches
who believe their own press releases and who have never sold
technology, by book authors who write what salespeople
want to hear, and by IT salespeople who struggle in their own
sales careers.

Selling IT is a managed process, where you, the salesperson,
must control the prospect's buying cycle. You can't be
subservient to prospects; they will abuse you every time, and
this will diminish your sales quota capture success.

Don't you have value, too?

Prospects don't know your value—only buyers do—so you
can't treat prospects the same as buyers.

To really grasp our concept and to be successful using the
Value Forward Sales method, you first must understand and

accept the following five IT sales fallacies. These five fallacies float around the sales training market space on a regular basis and clog the success factor of many salespeople. Understand and manage these five, and your sales closing ratio will immediately increase.

Fallacy Number One:
IT prospects always tell the truth.

If you have been an IT salesperson longer than 5 minutes, you know IT prospects do not tell the truth. They may not lie directly, but they exaggerate, misrepresent, don't know, or sometimes are just too embarrassed to tell you what is really going on in your sales cycle and in their buying environment. How many IT prospects have told you they make the decision, or they were not looking at anyone else, or they were going to buy "no later than Christmas"?

So, if you are talking with management prospects and are using their verbal communications as a benchmark of the progress of your sales cycle success—you are wasting your time.

Never believe what IT prospects say—focus on what they do!

Fallacy Number Two:
In IT sales, price is the most important buying criterion.

Wrong. Yes, price is important. But the buyer's job is to get the lowest price, and your job as an IT salesperson is to get the highest price. Price must equal value. So, if a prospect fails to believe your technology value conveyance—then your IT offering price is too high, and you have failed as a salesperson to communicate correctly your offering's business value.

When you buy a house, a car, or a boat, do you tell the salesperson that his or her price is right? Of course not! So, when a management buyer says your price is too high, don't assume it is—instead, think about how you can manage the value perception in the buyer's mind to get him or her to see and believe your price equals value.

In good economies and in bad, qualified prospects buy technology and professional services—when price equals value.

Fallacy Number Three: Prospects always check your IT references.

IT prospects are lazy. Hoping your prospects are going to help you sell them by calling your references is just projected expectation and idleness on your part. When prospects ask for five references, they call none. When they ask for 10 references, they call one. Never build your IT sales deal success (or sales forecast) based on the prospect's verbal commitment to perform purchase due diligence. Most prospects, regardless of title, do not know how to buy your technology or services correctly.

It's your commission. Manage it. Don't let the buyer control your income.

Fallacy Number Four:
Prospects buy brand on the first interaction.

Brand selling is a dominant IT sales methodology for Global 1000 sales teams, which are told by their marketing departments to tell prospects "Who we are." Brand selling to new IT prospects is the worst way to sell. Why? Because prospects are not educated buyers, and they will jump to brand conclusions about your business value based on what they think they know or don't know about your firm. If a prospect sits next to someone at a trade show and that person bad mouths your company, when you call a week later, the most recent "visual brochure" about you in that prospect's brain will be what was said about your firm at the trade show.

Why did NCR change its corporate brand name from National Cash Register? Because ATMs became one of its largest profit centers at the time.

Why did AT&T change its name from American Telephone and Telegraph? Because the company hasn't sold telegraphs in 150 years.

What does IBM sell? Cash registers, consulting, wiring, mainframes, laptops, ecommerce strategy—not just business machines! What you buy from IBM will depend on what you know and what you don't know about IBM …

… and that's the reason brand selling to new prospects reduces your IT selling success. Prospects may not be as educated as you think they are.

When selling <u>new</u> IT prospects, always focus on **Value First—Brand Second**.

Fallacy Number Five:
In IT sales, you have a relationship with the prospect before the first sale.

O.K., let's talk about the holy grail of IT sales—relationship selling. Relationship selling is the biggest fallacy most sales training books and sales coaches teach to IT salespeople. This perception holds back your IT sales success, elongates your sales cycle, wastes your selling time, and gives you false sales success indicators as you move through your sales cycle steps.

In IT sales, you do not have a relationship with a prospect until after the second sale.

Do you want to be a rich IT salesperson?

Do you want to be the top player in your company or industry?

Then focus on this observation, and let me repeat this:

In IT sales, you do not have a relationship with a prospect until after the second sale.

Here is what happens in IT sales. You have your first meeting with your targeted prospect—this is called the pre-sales cycle. At this step, you convey to the targeted prospect your business value. From this first meeting forward, you take your prospect through multiple activities where at some point he or she starts to believe your price equals value.

Then the prospect buys. This is the first transactional step.

After your buyer has installed your technology or used your professional services, this new customer goes into a post-

17

sales analysis to determine if the value received in the first transactional step is equal to what you, the salesperson, promised in the pre-sales cycle.

If the value is equal to or exceeds what you said the buyer would receive, and this customer buys from you a second time, then this person has started a relationship with you.

If during the post-sales cycle analysis, the IT buyer believes your product or service does not match up to what you described during the pre-sales cycle, your new customer will buy from someone else the second time.

Prospects buy a second time from the same vendor only when the risks are fewer than buying from a new vendor.

So, why are so many it salespeople so in love with the concept of relationship selling?

This concept of relationship selling appeals to the right-brain, feel-good, emotional side of salespeople because they have the perception that visibility, appointments being kept, friendly dialogue, and good verbal communication in an account will equal sales. Having lunch, meeting repeatedly at trade shows, doing demos, submitting multiple proposals, or having IT prospects take your calls does not mean you have a relationship with them.

Look at your sales pipeline right now.

Do you have any prospects in your pipeline who never left? Do you simply move these prospects to the next quarter because you still think they are going to buy from you based on your current "relationship?" Do their buy dates seem to be postponed quarter to quarter? Do you have any prospects in your sales pipelines who are always available to chat with you, who tell you at trade shows "You're the one"—who just don't buy?

Have you ever lost a deal to a competitor after spending a disproportionate amount of time with the targeted prospect, doing demo after demo, spec after spec, proposal after proposal, and yet this customer buys from someone else?

These are all symptoms you are using a relationship selling approach—which does not work for new sales.

The word *relationship* is defined as "a state of connectedness between people (especially an emotional connection)."

Do you have an emotional connection with an IT prospect who has never bought from you before?

Of course not.

Yet relationship sales training courses teach this fallacy every day to unsuspecting IT salespeople who believe it's the proven method for them to hit or exceed their assigned sales quotas. Sure, if you hang on to a prospect in a "relationship" long enough, he or she will move from a looking sales cycle step to a buying sales cycle step, but in IT sales, you don't have that time or luxury.

I remember getting an email from a *High Tech Success* (www.HighTechSuccess.com) newsletter subscriber named Ben who said, "Paul, you have it all wrong. Relationship selling is the key to IT sales success. I sold my biggest deal ever, a $3.2 million sale after working with my prospect for three years."

I sent a reply email and said, "Ben, congratulations, during those three years, did you ever hit your annual sales quota?"

I did not hear back from him for four weeks. When he finally replied, Ben said, "No, I missed it by 30 to 40 percent each year."

So, I responded with, "That's the point—to hit your annual IT sales quota (or exceed it) consistently, you must focus on prospects that are in the buying cycle now. You're lucky to still have your job, because most VPs of sales would have fired you."

Prospects don't have to like you, or invite you to their daughter's wedding, or buy you dinner to buy from you. So, stop building imaginary relationship bridges in your mind, convincing yourself that visibility and interaction in a targeted prospect account is going to help you sell more. Prior to the first sale, relationship selling is a seller's need—not a buyer's need.

Prospects are only interested in how your IT offerings will help them … that's it.

The 3T Sales Process

In today's crazy economy, to get targeted prospects to buy your technology or services, you need to use the 3T process of **trust, transactional selling**, and **time management**. When integrated together, this process increases your IT sales—all are needed, and they must work in tandem.

#1—Trust

In IT Sales, It's Trust—Not Relationships

Relationship selling is not needed to sell IT—but trust communicated by the seller and believed by the buyer is. The word "Trust" is defined as: "assured reliance on the character, ability, strength, or truth of someone or something."

So, it is important not to confuse the buyer's need for trust with the seller's desire to have a relationship.

Buyers must trust you. That is how they manage their risks (or perception of risks) that they may buy the wrong IT or buy from the wrong company. The buyer's trust is a need that must be fulfilled during your IT sales process, both by communication and education of your technology value and by your behavior, to get a management buyer to take an action step to purchase your IT offering.

Take the IT Trust Test

Here is a quick trust assessment you can take to determine if your prospect trusts you and your company.

1. Do prospects ask you for references more than 50 percent of the time?
   ☐ Yes   ☐ No

2. Do prospects ask you as a vendor to put all of your verbal commitments in writing?
   ☐ Yes   ☐ No

3. Do prospects ask for a written guarantee or a performance clause?

☐ Yes ☐ No

4. Are more than 50 percent of your leads and referrals from happy customers?

☐ Yes ☐ No

5. Have prospects told you privileged information during your IT sales cycle that is company confidential?

☐ Yes ☐ No

6. Do prospects and existing customers ask you for advice on complicated or delicate subjects?

☐ Yes ☐ No

7. Do prospects talk to you like a peer (instead of a vendor)?

☐ Yes ☐ No

8. Do your prospects ask to meet with your management team as a condition to buy from you?

☐ Yes ☐ No

9. Do prospects question the ability of your company to deliver your offering's strategic results?

☐ Yes ☐ No

10. Do prospects ask for extended payment terms with condition of payment attachments?

☐ Yes ☐ No

Correct Answers:

1) No	2) No	3) No	4) Yes	5) Yes
6) Yes	7) Yes	8) No	9) No	10) No

Scoring:

Each correct answer is worth 10 percent. How did you score? Is your score above 70 percent? If not, you have not established trust with your prospects.

#2—Transactional Selling

Transactional selling is the key to increased IT sales from new prospects.

Using trust, transactional selling methods, and time management in tandem creates a success paradigm that generates IT sales, fast and often.

Transactional selling forces prospects to prove to you they are qualified buyers by taking action steps with you in tandem during your sales cycle. Time management is a key to IT sales quota success. Wasting time with prospects who are professional lookers and who give verbal commitments minimizes your income potential. So, during your entire sales cycle, you must continually force IT prospects to move forward with you and to prove to you they are not wasting your valuable selling time.

No one has a two-year IT sales quota—so you must focus your selling time on prospects who are in the buying cycle ... now (even in a complex selling environment).

Transactional selling forces prospects to take action steps with you based on your selling needs—not the buyer's perceptions of the purchase.

To sell more IT, rely on transactional action steps—not verbal commitments.

Action steps you can ask your prospects to take to help prove to you they are qualified buyers in a purchase cycle include:

1. Giving you their exact budget number for their IT investment

2. Coming to your office to do a brick and mortar tour of your facilities

3. Introducing you to their boss

4. Visiting an existing client site with you

5. Giving you your competitor's proposal

6. Sending your contract to the legal department (Legal only looks at vendor contracts that are in the buy cycle; legal departments do not waste their time on vendors that are not short listed.)

7. Setting up an executive presentation with their C-level management team (Executives usually do not waste their time—so they won't waste your time.)

8. Signing a Letter of Intent (LOI) (An LOI has no real legal strength; it is purely a salesperson's tool to get the prospect to believe he or she has made a commitment to you and to tell your competitors to go away.)

9. Getting C-level prospects to confirm in front of their subordinates the date they want to be operational (Managers do not like to look foolish in front of their team members who work for them on a daily basis.)

Use these action steps as strategic drivers to create momentum in your sales process to confirm you're not wasting your time. It's one thing to lose a deal because you sold incorrectly; it's another to lose a deal because your "buyer" bought from no one and was only a professional looker.

In IT, there are only five reasons why prospects will buy from you—only four apply to business to business buyers. So, when trying to sell and market to qualified prospects, you must build your IT sales presentation based on these buyer drivers. Failure to focus on these drivers will cause your messaging to communicate your value incorrectly and will depress your revenue capture success.

Business to consumer buyers (B2C) acquire technology, software, or professional services based on one reason—how the technology purchase makes them feel. For example, purchases of electronic games drive you to be emotionally involved with the technology, creating happiness, suspense, fear, and satisfaction—sometimes all at the same time. Another example might be buying an iPad. Having an easy to carry tablet means your personal interests are readily available wherever you go, allowing you to feel independence and freedom from your home computer.

Business to business buyers (B2B) acquire technology, software, or professional services based on one (or all) of the following four reasons:

1. How your technology or professional service increases the buyer's income

2. How your technology or professional service decreases the buyer's expenses

3. How your technology or professional service manages the buyer's business risks or consequences

4. How your technology or professional service manages the buyer's business agility

If you do not correctly communicate your IT value to the targeted buyer, then that customer will never buy from you.

Depending on what type of technology, software, or professional services you sell, the four B2B drivers may be indirectly created for your buyers, and may not be as obvious to them during the sales cycle, causing them to slow down or even eliminate your sales cycle. So, when indirect buyer drivers are present, you must be aggressive, premeditated, and outbound in your description of these indirect outcomes, confirming for your buyers why they should buy.

Indirect IT Buyer Drivers

Indirect buyer driver examples for technology, software, and professional service purchases can include:

- Improved reporting that accelerates management decision making (report writer software, business intelligence applications, scorecards...)

- Increased operational business capabilities (technology tools and custom software development…)

- Improved staff productivity (customer relationship management (CRM), enterprise resource planning (ERP)…)

- Increased department capabilities (staff augmentation, project management…)

The goal of all IT prospect sales should be *transactional selling* first, *relationship selling* second.

Another IT Sales Training Mistake That Holds Back Most Salespeople

Have you attended a sales training course or read a sales book that says to sell a company, you must know intimately its business problems and the pains of the prospect you are trying to sell? This one theorem has launched tens of thousands of IT salespeople to aggressively study companies' websites, examine every word of these companies' press releases, and conduct weekend analysis of public companies' annual reports in hopes of discovering the centralized theme or the hidden need that will drive the IT buyer to buy.

What a waste of time!

The reason this is a waste of time is that management buys based on its verbal declaration of the business problems the company admits to, not necessarily the events being publicly discussed or disseminated in the company's marketing or by the press.

You could read in *The Wall Street Journal* the day of your first prospect appointment that your prospect's management team is losing $10 billion a year in manufacturing labor costs, and when you bring this up in your conversation with the senior vice president worldwide of manufacturing, your executive prospect will look you straight in the eye and say, "We have no labor cost problems!"

Why?

Because there is ego in the boardroom. To sell IT, you need to get the prospect to admit to a business problem before the company will pay for the solution. When you over study a company's individual issues before you talk with your prospects, you develop preconceived, biased perceptions of which business problems the company is prepared to pay to have fixed through the use of your IT products or services. Then, during your preliminary conversations with your prospects, you focus on what you "know" they "need" based on your research and company knowledge.

This is called seller's ego.

Just like buyer's ego, seller's ego must be managed during the sales process for IT sales to increase. The prospects don't care about you and what you know. They don't even care about your technology. To your buyers, technology is just a business tool to drive results. All they care about are their needs and specifically the business problems they have and will openly admit to.

This "over study" sales approach is very common in Global 1000 IT firms that sell key accounts. They have their sales pursuit teams huddle together to discuss their targeted prospects' known business events to "align" their technology offerings to help them sell faster. All this does is elongate their sales cycles and overcomplicate an already complex selling environment.

That's why it is easy to beat Global 1000 IT sales teams. They all use ego-driven sales processes based on their needs ... not the buyers'. All they talk about is their company's "brand," "their knowledge" of the prospect's business problems, and how "they" can help the company.

During a public seminar I held in Boston, with 150 people in the room, a Global 50 regional sales vice president, responsible for more than 1,000 salespeople, stood up and said, "At the end of the quarter, when I am trying to help my team try to close a huge deal, all we can do is drop our price because all the Global 50 IT companies we compete against are basically the same!"

That's the point. Most IT firms do not know how to communicate their business value specifically and correctly to their targeted buyers. They don't know how to be a truly strategic advisor that helps prospects see their business value three dimensionally, so they end up using a discounted price as a sales objection management tool to close business. If they stopped being so seller-ego-driven and actually focused on their buyers' needs (instead of their own), they would sell more at higher margins.

In IT sales, it's not about you. Prospects don't care about you or your technology or what you think are the reasons they will buy. It's all about them and their needs, specifically the needs they admit to. So, taking up your valuable selling time at the beginning of your sales cycle with specific prospect problem analysis before they admit to their needs and business issues is unproductive, and it wastes your time.

You don't sell technology or software or professional services—you sell the results your IT produces. Specifically you sell IT that fixes the business problems your buyers admit to.

So, stop spending valuable selling time over studying your targeted prospects before you know if they are qualified; instead (as I will teach you later), focus on knowing the common business problems in their industry and getting the target prospects to admit to the problems they will pay for— the ones (you hope) your IT offerings fix.

To Sell More IT, Sell Executive Management

When trying to identify your ideal technology buyer, executive management becomes the most obvious choice for salespeople seeking to exceed their sales quotas.

So, why do so many IT salespeople not sell to executives? Why do so many IT salespeople take the path of least resistance and sell to lower prospect contacts? It's because they don't know how to get to executive management—and they believe that any entry point into an organization is better than no forward momentum.

They are wrong.

To sell more IT and to become a rich salesperson, you must focus on the executive management level as your first entry point into a targeted account.

What title qualifies as executive management? In North America, targeted business titles to sell technology and services should be vice presidents and above. Outside of

North America, titles like director and general manager are more appropriate.

Why sell vice presidents and above?

When selling technology, there are two precise selling zones in North America that must be understood and managed. Each IT selling zone has its own unique operating characteristics, behavioral buying patterns, and environmental conditions.

IT Selling Zone One – The Commodity Selling Zone-Controlled

This zone is populated by employees who hold business titles that include director, manager, system analyst, and network administrator. They control your sales process and perception of business value.

IT Selling Zone Two – The Value Selling Zone-Uncontrolled

This selling zone comprises executives who hold the titles of vice president, managing director, CFO, CIO, COO, and CEO. These leadership managers do not control your sales process, and they allow you to manage their perception of your technology or professional service value.

Zone One buyers make technology buying decisions based on your offering's features, functions, price, or professional service deliverables. That's their realm of reference to make a judgment call to decide if your IT offering meets their needs. This selling zone is often a tightly structured environment that has little leeway for negotiation outside of these four buyer driver variables. Zone One buyers often generate the Request For Proposals (RFPs) and Request For Information

(RFIs) to which most IT companies respond, input hundreds of man-hours, and then lose.

Zone Two buyers make technology, software, and service buying decisions based <u>on their perception of the value of your IT or service offering</u> *you create.*

This distinction gives you, the thinking, premeditated IT salesperson, the ability to penetrate the no-talk zone of management because you can manipulate the Zone Two executive managers' perceptions of value. Value is a variable, observational belief—different for each of us based on our education, researched knowledge, IT offering expectations, business experiences, company market model, and selling process.

In Zone One, buyers are looking for features, functions, and price. Your IT offering has what they want, or it doesn't. Your price is too high, or it isn't. And on any given day, when you are selling in Zone One, your IT offering can be behind in its features, function, and deliverables based on how aggressively your competitors are prepared to develop product or give it away. So, marketing in the Commodity Selling Zone is a waste of time.

By selling to vice presidents and above in Zone Two, your IT offering's value is based on the perception of what the buyer believes, and so you gain competitive flexibility. When done correctly, you can reposition your IT offering's value, even when it's non-competitive with the buyer's other options and price expectations. By changing the visual brochure in the mind of the executive, you can win more deals at a greater price point because price must equal value, and when it does—budgets get found or enlarged.

So, why do so many IT salespeople sell to directors and below?

Selling in the Commodity Selling Zone is common for many IT salespeople because it is an easy entry point into any organization. Directors and below are professional lookers who steal your valuable selling time and reduce your sales quota attainment success. They will take a vendor appointment anytime—just to make themselves look busy to the boss.

Can you sell IT and professional services to directors and below? Of course, but it extends your sales cycle timeline and forces you to have your sales commissions and sales success managed by a nonprofessional communicator who becomes a liaison between you and the decision maker. When selling in Zone One, you are asking your IT sales wealth to be negotiated by non-salespeople. Selling IT is hard enough; do you really want a non-salesperson to handle the discussion of your company's value, price, or Q&A on how you are different from your competitors with the buyer who signs the contract?

So, again, why do so many IT salespeople sell in the Commodity Selling Zone? Because it is easy, and most don't know how to sell in the Value Selling Zone, so they take the path of least resistance.

Sell value, not features and functions. Sell to buyers who want value, not to buyers who digest 100-page operational manuals.

As we continue to build our sales tool box with concepts and approaches, one question that may arise is how to decide to which buyer (title) you should sell your IT. Yes, selling to C-level executives is a key driver to sell more, but should the type of technology or service you sell be sold in Zone Two? Do you sell technology tools to CFOs? Do you sell website development tied to a backend customer database to the CEO?

To determine which entry position is most logical for the type of technology or service you sell, take the sales proportionality test.

The IT Sales Proportionality Test

The sales proportionality test says the dollar value of your first IT sale must be proportionate to the business title value of the person to whom you are selling. For example, if you are selling a $400,000.00 ERP application to a director of a $20 million manufacturing company, the price of your IT offering is too high. A $400K IT decision in a $20M company is made by the CFO or maybe even the CEO.

Additionally, if you are trying to sell a $1 million IT project management package to a CEO of a $20 billion public company, then this targeted entry point is also wrong. Divisional general managers or senior vice presidents in public companies of this size usually make that level of investment decision.

If you're trying to sell in the IT Value Selling Zone and are having trouble penetrating the company's organizational chart, it may be the price of what you sell is too low. One of my consulting clients was a $49 million, West Coast application provider selling to the manufacturing industry. For years, this company struggled to get into the Value Selling Zone and regularly changed its marketing, strategy, and sales process in an attempt to rectify this issue. We came in, did a Value Forward 360-degree high tech business assessment and success recommendation program and discovered that our client's current marketing, selling process, pricing methods, and business strategy were holding this company back. The first thing we did was raise its software app price 30 percent. That's right—we raised pricing 30 percent. Then we changed the corporate messaging and custom fit our client's marketing and sales training approach (the *Value Forward Sales* method), and within 97 days, this company increased its C-suite market penetration on the first call by over 67 percent, shortened the sales cycle selling time by 3½ months, increased margins by 48 percent, and drove top line revenue up by 29 percent year over year for three straight years. Magic? Hard to believe? No, not really. The business title to whom you sell dictates the price and messaging of what you sell.

Important IT sales success variables to remember:

- If you want to sell higher in an organizational chart, change your messaging and raise your pricing.

- If you want to increase your gross margin, sell higher in the organizational chart, where price is not as relevant.

- Gross margin size is tied to the size of your sales pipeline. The smaller the pipeline, the more you are apt to discount.

- IT sales is not selling—it is explaining your value.

- When you demo your IT early in the sales cycle, you are unintentionally turning your sale into a commodity, so postpone your IT sales demo as long as possible. First, spend more time asking questions about the prospects' needs and explaining how your IT increases their income, decreases their expenses, manages their business risks or consequences, and helps them increase their business agility.

- Your first entry point into a new prospect company's organizational chart dictates how that prospect sees you. Enter too low, and even before you speak or provide a proposal, you are already in commodity.

#3—Time Management

To sell more, to increase your sales quota success, you must manage your selling time, time management. You can sell $2 million in 12 months or 36 months. The success driver in exceeding your assigned sales quota within your company's fiscal year is working with qualified buyers not professional lookers.

It is up to you. Prospects who are qualified IT buyers always take action steps with you in tandem (transactional selling) to prove to you that they are active participants in your sales process.

Don't hope that lookers will act like buyers.

Hope is not a sales strategy.

Chapter

2

Positioning Your Message (Brand) to Sell More IT

After reading this section, you will learn:

- How to develop a unique Sales Value Proposition

- How to paint a picture that makes executives listen

- How to become an industry guru in any business market

Perception Is Reality—Branding Is Not

Branding by most IT companies is a wasted effort. If your brand is confusing or requires too much buyer education, you end up with reduced revenue. So, to increase your success in the Value Selling Zone with your targeted prospects, you must build a technology sales approach and a value message. Communicating value to management buyers will make them listen and ultimately take action steps to buy.

When selling technology services and software, the key to penetrating the no talk door of management prospects in the Value Selling Zone is your company's positioning and messaging statement. In the digital economy, we hear quite a bit about company branding and the correct way to position your firm, but the best way for your account manager and marketing departments to sell technology in volume is to develop a unique Sales Value Proposition (SVP) that is **truly <u>only</u> yours**.

Most brand messaging is created by marketing agencies' account managers who have not carried an IT sales bag or sold against entrenched Global 100 competitors. Branding in its traditional design is often a wasted model of value creation because it becomes too nebulous for new buyers to understand and just forces IT salespeople into a rigid, identification defined box. So, to increase value communications to a qualified prospect, use SVPs.

SVPs are not Unique Selling Propositions (USPs) or branding tag lines. According to Wikipedia, USP is a marketing concept first proposed as a theory to explain a pattern among successful advertising campaigns of the early 1940s. Such campaigns made unique propositions to customers, and those propositions convinced buyers to switch brands.

SVPs are specifically reconstructed messages—based on your buyers' needs—that communicate directly to prospects why they should buy from you.

Most IT companies spend more time communicating their technical knowledge than packaging their value. It's not what you know—it's how buyers see and "believe" your IT can help them.

Trying to sell to a Fortune 1000 or a small business owner requires getting your company's value message through the volume of inbound salespeople that senior executives in small and large companies are exposed to week in and week out.

When talking with prospects, you must craft precise language that will stimulate them to take an action step to listen. Management prospects will make a quick judgment about you and your offering based on their past experiences with other salespeople and how you speak. You can be a graduate of Harvard, have an MBA from the Wharton School of Finance, and be making $500K per year as a great IT salesperson, but as soon as your management prospects hear you as a vendor trying to sell them technology, they're going to assign you that position in their minds. Now you are like every other salesperson they have met (think car, insurance, and real estate), and you are just wasting their time.

If you talk like a peer—they will treat you like a peer.

If you talk like a vendor—they will treat you like a vendor.

So, when communicating your firm's business values, don't just say, "We are North Shore Software Development, Hilman Consulting, or Data Keyboard Systems Integration Group Inc." or *"We market software to manufacturing companies."* Instead, think more strategically. Position yourself differently.

Get through the noise.

Communicate your value. Value drives prospects to take action steps to listen and ultimately to buy.

Your SVP should appeal to the Value Selling Zone executive and the specific vertical business industry in which you are trying to sell. If you are calling on the president of a 100-person company or the CFO of a Fortune 50, you need to think like this person does. Ask yourself, what are the business problems the industry is facing on a daily basis? How does your IT offering increase this company's income, decrease its expenses, manage its business risks or consequences, or improve its business agility?

As discussed before, we do not want to "over study" the prospect's "individual" company business issues, but instead we want to become knowledgeable about the business vertical industry problems as a whole. Later, I will teach you how to use your industry knowledge as a business lever to position yourself as a specialist.

The Five Guidelines to Crafting Successful IT Sales Value Propositions That Open Doors

1. Keep your SVPs short and succinct—seven words or fewer.

2. Always use the word "specialist" (not "expert") in your SVP.

3. Always describe in your SVP how your IT or professional service increases income, decreases expenses, and/or manages business risks or consequences for the buyer.

4. Never use a technology term in your SVP. IT words are commodity words, and you want to communicate

value. Remember, you don't sell technology; you sell the results of what your IT does.

5. Always include in your SVP the vertical business industry in which you are trying to sell.

If your firm specializes in selling technology to a specific vertical, try to use that industry's name in your SVP's description (e.g., Specialists in Casino Player Retention, etc.).

If your firm sells technology to a broad horizontal market, be more generic in your SVP's description (e.g., Recurring Revenue Stream Management Specialists for the X Industry, etc.).

Often in the IT market space, management teams automatically place themselves into commodity when they create their value statements by adapting established technology category acronyms to describe what they sell. CRM, VT, ECRM, and ERP are all well-established technology monikers, and their characteristics for pricing, features, functions, and value are already developed in the minds of buyers. To say you have a new, unique VT offering means nothing and just diminishes your sales cycle selling success. You and 100 other companies!

When you sound the same, act the same, and price the same as your competition, you are the same—and you have entered the Commodity Selling Zone.

Instead, create a new category of one. Use your SVP as a messaging "poker play" that makes prospects listen.

Here are some examples of technology, software, and professional service SVPs I have developed for clients. All of them have been successful, and all of them are for IT companies.

- Specialists in Inventory Personalization Controls for the Retail Industry

- Migration Management Specialists for the Hotel Industry

- Transaction Business Specialists for the X Industry

- Profit Improvement Specialists for the X Industry

- Retail Customer Lifetime Value Management Specialists

- Guest Retention Management Specialists for the Restaurant Industry

- Web Connectivity Management Specialists for the Health Care Industry

- Cruise Ship Guest Revenue Management Specialists

- Business Development Architects for Technology Companies

- Theme Park Employee Retention Management Specialists

- Hospitality Profitability Improvement Specialists

Always shoot for a term that is not currently used in your industry but addresses a benefit important to your industry. You can borrow terms from other industries. **Just be different!**

How to Test Your Sales Value Proposition's Uniqueness

Once you have crafted your SVP, search Google to see if another firm (in and out of your industry) is using it. If not, you have created a new value statement you can test with prospects.

If your SVP is already in use in your market, you may want to change it because the visual brochure in the mind of the buyer may already be set, and this SVP may put you into conformity just by its use.

How to Become an Industry Guru for Any Business Market in 10 Minutes or Less

So, how do you as an IT salesperson sell multiple industries and position your communication (and SVP) as a business specialist to Value Selling Zone targeted prospects—without wasting all your valuable selling time reading tomes of business journals and doing market research?

It's easy. Here's the secret sauce. Go to the vertical industry association website of the business in which you are trying to sell, for example, the National Chemical Association, the National Manufacturing Association, or the National Hospitality Association. Print out 10 to 15 pages of the website and circle all the words you don't know. Collect these words and look them up on the Internet and build a buyer's dictionary of industry terms. Then go back to the association's national website and download the annual trade show brochure and write down the titles of the trade show's breakout sessions and seminars. These titles are the business problems of this industry.

How do I know?

Because every association serves its members and tries to address its industry's problems at the annual trade show by hosting informative, educational breakout sessions. So, as an industry specialist, you can easily quote industry problems to any targeted management prospect as stated by the prospect's industry association, without concern that you are inaccurate.

A study was done several years ago to find out where senior level executives gain their technology and business information. The study revealed that managers gather 77 percent of their technology and business knowledge **FROM VENDORS**—people like you and me. The research behind this information indicates that most executives are just too busy to read all the trade publications in their market. So, they rely on vendors to keep them up-to-date.

This fact alone means executives are always looking for that newest business process to make them successful. This means when you call prospects with your SVP, they will want to know more—if they have never heard of it before. But if your SVP message is shallow and unoriginal, it will fail, and the prospect will not take your call.

When selling executive management, remember that fear has no budget. So, when you're crafting a sales value proposition, try as much as possible to describe how your IT offering manages business risks or business consequences.

At times, the SVP you create may be different from your company's generic value proposition statement. I have used this approach with **EVERY** technology and professional services firm I **have ever worked for, managed, consulted with, or owned. It always works.** So, when crafting your SVP, *__never be a generalist; always be a specialist__*.

When I was a new IT salesperson, I developed my own presentations and telemarketing scripts to reinforce my SVP. Later, when I became a vice president of sales and marketing and then a company founder, I implemented my unique SVPs companywide. Developing your SVP early will help you generate more appointments, make unique presentations, and close a greater percentage of technology sales. Being different causes key decision makers to **LISTEN.**

Case History – Hotel Reservations Technology

Earlier in my IT sales career, I was head hunted by some venture capitalists into a position as a vice president of sales and marketing for a hotel software and services company with annual revenues of $20+ million. Our average sale ranged from $400,000.00 to over $1 million and included software, hardware, training, and support. Our market was worldwide, and we had many competitors with newer versions of technology software trying to win our clients. When I was hired, I was told we would be deploying the updated version of our software within the next six months. As it often happens in privately funded companies, development slowed. Instead of having the new application in six months, the delivery date slipped to 18 months.

What could I do? The CEO said no new money was available for development, my 10 account sales managers were complaining they were losing deals to competitors with better software, and the board of directors kept asking me "Where are your sales revenues we expect your department to generate?" (Does this sound familiar?)

Here is what I reasoned. Since our application was a mature product and our competitors' applications were Version 1 on new platforms, we held the upper hand in deploying a functionality-rich software program. The key at that point was to position our SVP around our strengths: how we helped prospects increase their business success and how my competitors didn't. Here are the steps I took to achieve this objective:

Step 1 After doing some guerilla marketing on our competitors' feature sets, I discovered their applications (both old versions and new ones) were weak on customer service and their ability to track guests' lifetime value in the hotel reservations area. That's where our application excelled.

Step 2 Doing additional research on my prospects, I discovered guest management is always a big issue for hotels. Knowing that, I developed a complete SVP based on this one area.

Step 3 I created a new industry term called **"Guest Retention Management Specialists."**

Step 4 I wrote a white paper on the concept and got it published in several trade publications.

Step 5 I developed custom PowerPoint presentations and company brochures to match my marketing.

Step 6 I developed a verticalized telemarketing script to cold call hotel executives (the general manager of single locations, the vice president of operations of chains) about our unique services.

Step 7 I created a specialized sales presentation on how we were **Guest Retention Management Specialists**.

With our new SVP in place, my sales team and I attacked the market and our competitors, and we increased sales quarter over quarter.

Since this was in the early 1990s, CRM systems were not even invented yet, so our **Guest Retention Management** systems for hotels became a hit.

* * *

As you can see, I was a Rhino (see Chapter 1). Instead of caving in and whining like a Cow in response to sales and management pressure, I developed a unique SVP to beat my IT competitors.

I made up a new SVP that the executives were curious to hear about and my competitors couldn't compete against. How could they? I made it up! It was different, and it worked.

In this case, I created the market perception and made it a reality.

So, what happened? Sales went up 27 percent the first year, even though we were marketing old technology.

Perception Is Reality

Case History – Professional and Internet Services

While working for another company as a vice president, I was asked to launch a new division that sold business development consulting, web development, technology project work, managed services, and technology staffing to new economy companies.

Knowing this market space was overwhelmed with thousands of competitors in the United States, I knew I would have to develop a unique SVP to compete and succeed.

Using the seven steps of the SVP program I had developed, I implemented another new marketing campaign, as follows:

Step 1 I researched my competitors and discovered they were focused on selling singular services one at a time, usually to the company's CIO.

Step 2 I researched my prospects and discovered the CEOs of these new economy start-ups were spending a disproportionate amount of their business time raising venture capital funding and managing their investors' expectations. These expectations and the business control clauses usually written into the contracts CEOs sign when they receive funding from venture capitalists are called "milestones" and "ratchets."

Step 3 I created a new industry term called **"Milestone Management Specialists."**

Step 4 I wrote a white paper on this concept and got it published.

Step 5 I developed a custom PowerPoint presentation, marketing collateral, and a website to complement our SVP.

Step 6 I developed a verticalized telemarketing script to cold call CEOs who recently had received investor funding to discuss our **Milestone Management** services.

Step 7 I created a specialized in-person sales presentation to communicate our **Milestone Management** program. I also developed SVP talking points that highlighted my services' ability to increase revenues and reduce expenses.

So, what happened? My business development managers and I cold called CEOs of new economy companies, scheduled in-person appointments, and closed 50 percent of those deals on the first contact. Yes, that's correct—**50 percent**. Once we got in front of the CEOs as Milestone Management Specialists, we talked about "helping them increase their business valuation and funding opportunities by supplying them services that would help them meet their milestones on time and under budget."

Of course, these services were web development, application development, business consulting, and technology staffing— identical to all of our competitors' services. We were successful because we were attacking the pain of CEOs with a top-down approach, selling our services to meet their needs (which were the milestone and ratchet clauses in their venture capitalism contracts). Concurrently, we were bypassing our competitors who were calling on the CIOs.

By using this SVP method, we were able to beat out well-established Fortune 500 services and technology companies because their major account sales forces were focused on communicating generic-sounding company positioning and branding statements.

<u>We sounded different</u>. <u>We acted different</u>. <u>And we got the business</u>.

You are probably starting to notice a pattern. The key is to be different from everyone else. If you are like me, you always seem to be meeting larger and more established competitors. If you push against your competitors, you will lose. Instead, use stealth, like a Navy Seal. Evaluate your competition and prospects, determine what weapons you will use, and under the cover of night, attack and destroy.

Perception is reality.

Be unique. Develop a new market position, package it, and then communicate your story to the world and the key decision makers.

Paint your picture in the mind of the buyer!

* * *

Q: How do you develop your SVP?

A: The key is to plan your approach and to follow these seven steps:

Step 1   Study your competition. It is *not* what you sell. It is *who* you sell against.

Step 2   Research your targeted customers' industry business needs. What is their pain? What are the words and vernacular of their industry?

Step 3   Develop a new concept or industry term. Be creative and use industry terms based on your customers' vernacular.

Step 4   Write a white paper on your new concept and push to get it published.

Step 5   Develop a PowerPoint presentation and marketing collateral to match your new concept.

Step 6   Develop a telemarketing script to match your new concept.

Step 7   Create an in-person sales presentation that matches your SVP.

Highlights of this section:

In this section, I introduced:

- The Sales Value Proposition (SVP)

- Seven steps to support your SVP

- Perception is reality

- Always be a specialist, never a generalist

Exercises:

1. Go to your prospects' industry trade association websites and identify their industry problems and use this information as a foundation of your SVP's construction.

2. Visit a local bookstore or the Internet and subscribe to at least one industry or executive magazine you have never read before. Highlight, copy, or remove pages that contain information you want to refer back to and place them in a file so you can reference the information easily.

3. Examine a product or a service you are selling. Develop an SVP on that product or service. Follow the seven steps and build your new marketing campaign.

Remember, in IT sales, perception is reality. SVPs create three-dimensional value on how your IT increases income, reduces expenses, or manages business risks for your targeted buyers. Use them as tools to improve your IT sales.

Chapter

3

Finding IT Clients and Penetrating Their No Talk Zone

After reading this section, you will learn:

- How to find technology prospects through cold calling and other lead generation techniques

- How to penetrate their barrier to entry

- How to set up appointments with decision makers

Sell Up, Never Down

In a world where corporate politics flourish even in the smallest company, knowing who signs the purchase order or contract is a major key to a successful technology sales process that is scalable and replicable.

Since the Internet has made technology a level playing field for many competitors, key decisions for technology acquisitions are now usually made by a broad spectrum of executive management titles, including, but not limited to:

- C-level (CIO, COO, CEO, CFO) and VP-level executives for Fortune 1000 sales

- President or owner for small business sales

As discussed before, the first mistake most technology salespeople make is calling on a prospect too low in the company's organizational chart. Salespeople get intimidated about selling to the highest level because of their fear of rejection. This fear stems from their inability to frame a strong SVP to a senior manager. Account managers usually push to get into a targeted company, and they accept any entry point to get traction. This is always the wrong move.

Let me repeat that. This is ALWAYS the wrong move.

If you are a CEO, a sales manager, or a company sales vice president in a technology company, focus on having all your sales account managers cold call ONLY VPs and above.

Remember, no matter how big the company is, managers and directors almost never have the authority to sign off on business proposals. Even when they tell you it is their decision, they are still going to go ask the boss. Another interesting observation in technology sales is that managers and directors never send you up to their bosses—only down to their subordinates.

When was the last time a director of IT or operations said to you "I love your technology. Let me introduce you to my boss, the vice president"?

It doesn't happen.

Directors and managers either bring your opportunity directly to their bosses and try to make themselves look good by explaining your value based on how they understand it, or they send you to George, the program manager. Either way, you lose. The director or manager is not as good a salesperson as you are and will likely communicate your message in the wrong way to the vice president, handle the FAQ poorly, or worse, refer you down to George, who cannot make any decisions.

Always sell up—the higher, the better. Always try to sell to business executives, not technical people.

If you have crafted your SVP correctly, and if your IT offering passes the price proportionality test, you should be able to cold call the C-level executive of a Global 1000 and get his or her attention. Having the CEO send you down to the senior vice president of operations worldwide is a whole lot better than talking to George, the program manager.

Case History – Global 1000 Selling Up

Recently, I taught an experienced director of business development how to cold call the CEO of a Fortune 1000 company. Using the SVP script, he reached the CEO's administrator and left a message with her.

The CEO's secretary called back and said the CEO was interested and wanted the technology salesperson to call the senior vice president of marketing. The account manager called the VP and told him the CEO was interested and had instructed him to set up an appointment to chat. Of course, the senior vice president of marketing said yes.

If the technology salesperson had cold called lower in the organizational chart, he may never have gotten the chance to meet the senior vice president of marketing.

To sell more, avoid CIOs—when you can.

Another important sales concept you should consider when you sell IT is that **many technology investments are not IT decisions, but business decisions**. CIOs today have larger technology budgets than ever before, but they also have less control, so if you are trying to sell—try to avoid selling to CIOs as much as possible. CIOs manage in most cases a staff position department that is a cost center. Strategically, when making your first entry point into a targeted prospect company within the Value Selling Zone, try to work with line position executives whose departments make money. These targeted executive should hold titles like VP of sales, VP of marketing, VP of business operations, VP of engineering, VP of finance, VP of operations, or CFO/COO/CEO.

Twenty years ago, a CEO would never ask the CIO if the corporate infrastructure was going to be running on a SaaS app or an ERP system. But today, VPs of operations, VPs of marketing, CMOs, and of course, CEOs all have direct budgets and/or direct influences on which technology is acquired for their company. Technology today (depending on its value) is a boardroom decision. Always sell to the highest level in the organizational chart based on your offering's proportionality.

Aim Low—End Low.

So, when prospecting, aim high.

Case History – SaaS Accounting Company

A privately held SaaS accounting company I consulted with recently had been cold calling the director of marketing of a small 25-person business without much success. I suggested the technology salesperson call the CEO with a special SVP based on the value (increasing income, decreasing expenses, managing risks, or improving agility) the company's technology offered. The salesperson did this and got a meeting.

Many times, in both large and small companies, lower-level managers, who often are motivated by politics, will prevent you from getting to the decision maker. So, focus on the right title, craft the right message, and you will increase your success.

Additionally, sometimes an SVP is intellectually over the heads of lower-level employees. Senior managers of any size firm generally have broader knowledge about their business and their operational needs than department supervisors, and so using an SVP on a lower-level manager in the Commodity Selling Zone is often a waste of time.

So, stop wasting your time with low level manager titles.

Sell up, never down.

In the *Value Forward Sales* method, a lead or a contact is not considered a prospect unless the person has a title of vice president or above, has a budget, and shows action steps to buy. If you follow this method, you will sell more technology.

Go for the heavy hitters, and you will become a heavy hitter.

*The successful person has the habit of doing
the things failures don't like to do. They don't
like doing them either necessarily. But their
disliking is subordinated to the strength of
their purpose. –E. M. Gray*

*Technology: No Place for Wimps! –Scott
Adams*

Cold Calling—How to Increase Your IT Sales Success Factor Immediately

***This is the area that separates a professional IT salesperson
making $500,000.00 a year from everyone else.***

There are only three ways to generate IT sales leads, only
three! Networking, marketing, and cold calling. There is no
magic secret. As a professional IT salesperson, you must
include all these methods in your lead generation programs.
But you must focus on cold calling in your arsenal as a
primary tool to be successful. Should the marketing
department generate leads for the IT sales team? Of course.

But you can't wait for that department to generate business
for you. It's your responsibility to hit your assigned sales
quota, within the environment in which you operate. So, if
your marketing department is all talk and no show—don't
wait for it.

Networking does work. As an experienced IT salesperson,
you need to seek out every referral you can generate.
LinkedIn is, by far, the best social network tool for IT
salespeople. Used correctly, you can build a referral base

directly and indirectly that will lead you to contact opportunities that may be three to five degrees of separation from you.

Networking, however, offers you only a limited replicable lead generation program. Just because you know someone or are introduced to someone does not mean this person has an IT buying demand or budget. So, once you exhaust all your networking opportunities, and the leads from your marketing department dry up, what are you going to do?

Successful IT salespeople prosper within the environment in which they operate.

You have a choice. Do nothing or cold call. Ultimately, cold calling becomes a primary lead generation program for IT salespeople who truly want to succeed.

If you cannot or will not cold call, *you will not make large sums of money.*

Professional IT salespeople always cold call. Cold calling is the fastest way to increase your sales pipeline, your company's revenue, and your personal income. It is the difference between making an appointment with a CFO of a Global 1000 company or a CEO of a privately held $30 million firm and selling middle level managers. If you analyze the top income sales positions in the United States, such as stockbrokers, commercial insurance salespeople, or merger and acquisitions salespeople, you will find they all cold call. Salespeople who make cold calls are always better salespeople. Why? Because they set more appointments, which provide them more opportunities to practice their sales presentations and, ultimately, to generate more closed deals.

If you are one of those account managers who waits for the corporate marketing department to send you leads, odds are you will never be the top salesperson in your company on a repeat basis. Never.

Cold calling is the key to selling more technology.

Cold calling is the key to selling more SaaS.

Cold calling is the key to selling more professional services.

Cold calling is the key to selling more enterprise software.

* * *

Q: When is the best time to cold call?

A: All day.

* * *

Q: When will you be the most successful in getting to speak with C-level executives?

A: Before 8 a.m. and after 5:30 p.m. their time because the assistants are gone and the boss usually picks up his or her own phone.

* * *

I Am a Senior IT Salesperson—I Don't Cold Call

The fact is senior IT salespeople who don't cold call on a regular basis are actually junior salespeople in disguise. All professional IT salespeople cold call.

Why?

Because cold calling is the shortest path to peer-to-peer communication with targeted executives, and it allows senior IT salespeople to talk directly with management prospects.

Because my newsletter *High Tech Success* (www.hightechsuccess.com) is the largest IT sales and marketing success newsletter in the world, we get calls weekly from telemarketing firms saying they want us to recommend them. We tell everyone who calls to give us the names of between five and eight vice presidents of sales who will confirm the telemarketer's inside sales team sets up C-level appointments more than 75 percent of the time. Prove that to us, we tell them, and we will hand you our 600-plus IT client list we have worked with since 2001—free of charge.

No one ever calls back.

Why?

Because using an inside telemarketer or a third party cold calling firm as a communication intermediary diminishes your C-level prospecting. If the telemarketers had the same polished communication skills the senior salespeople they are calling for had, then they would be the outside senior IT salespeople, who are paid a lot more money.

Don't let junior salespeople present your brand to customers on the telephone; cold call yourself and establish a peer-to-peer interaction from the beginning of your premeditated sales cycle.

The smart way to cold call on the phone is to buy a targeted database of your prospects from a list company and load it into a CRM system like Sage Act, Siebel, Gold Mine, Microsoft Dynamics, or SalesForce.com.

Then, at least three times each week, make at least 30 calls each day prospecting for new business from new prospects. (The best way to cold call is to schedule cold calling time in your appointment book like an appointment with yourself.)

The first thing you may ask is *"How am I going to make 30 calls a day?"* You will not reach 30 people on a daily basis. Instead, you will speak with gatekeepers (more on this later) or get voice mail 80 percent of the time. The other 20 percent, you will be touching prospects, and with prospecting comes increased revenue and increased commissions (remember, target vice presidents or above).

* * *

Q: How many companies should you cold call?

A: Based on your market, you should load between 300 and 400 companies into your database. By cold calling at least 30 new companies a day, three days a week, you will end up contacting every company once a month.

* * *

Cold calling peer-to-peer's immediate effects:

1. Increases your sales pipeline's size

2. Builds your confidence in speaking with prospects

3. Shortens your sales cycles by falling into other IT competitors' sales cycles that are already under way

4. Increases the number of appointments you get with prospects

5. Enables you to negotiate better with prospects because you have multiple deals closing at the same time

6. Improves your sales skills because of increased prospect interactions

Keep in mind, most of your competitors do not like to cold call. Most "senior" salespeople will say it is beneath them. This lack of aggressive outbound "Hunt Now or Be Eaten Later!®" approach creates a gap of opportunity for those IT salespeople who seek to be more successful.

Here is an interesting side effect of cold calling. If there are five salespeople in your company, and they each call 400 companies a month, that is 2,000 companies hearing your name and getting your SVP message every month.

That's called advertising and branding!

Another benefit of cold calling is that you get better at selling. The more you talk to prospects, the more confident you become and the higher your close ratio will be. By implementing a cold calling program, your sales will go up.

* * *

Q: What is the best way to cold call Fortune 1000 companies?

A: Always cold call by phone.

* * *

Q: What is the best way to cold call small business owners?

A: When the small company has fewer than 20 employees, cold calling in person works well too. But in today's security conscious world, it is a lot harder to do, especially in large office buildings with security entrances.

* * *

Telemarketing and Cold Calling

Telemarketing Scripts

The key to making telemarketing work for you is seeing the results of your efforts. This means setting up appointments with qualified decision makers. These appointments could entail meeting with a senior vice president of marketing in a Fortune 200 company to discuss an Internet CRM system, sitting down with a CFO to chat about your enterprise software's value, or talking with a CEO of a 100-person bike manufacturer to discuss an assembly line software application to reduce unit construction costs.

Before you can write your telemarketing script, though, you need to develop your SVP.

Make sure your SVP answers or responds to your target's business problems or pains. Selling technology successfully means you are a "doctor." You need to identify the prospect's business pain he or she admits to and then fix it with your IT by closing the sale.

Your Telemarketing Objective

Your objective when telemarketing is to set up a 20-minute business introduction/qualification meeting on the phone or in person at a later date. Your goal is **not** to tell the IT prospect how great your firm is and to give him or her a one-hour feature/function description of your software or IT service offering on the first phone call.

If you spend more than eight minutes on your first telemarketing call, you are selling your IT. Sell the first appointment—not your technology.

Since 2001, when this book was originally published, I have received many emails and phone calls about the telemarketing script success plan I am about to give you. This plan will help you increase the success of your IT sales cold calling. I have had IT salespeople just like you use our nine-step telemarketing script and get CEOs of Fortune 1000 companies on the phone and sell technology or professional services to those firms.

Reasons Why This Telemarketing Script Will Not Work and How to Adjust

This script is very effective when used appropriately. But if you are not being successful, it is usually tied to three specific reasons:

1. You do not follow the nine steps of this script in progression. The telemarketing steps are designed to be used in a very specific, sequential process. This process contains psychology, competitive pressure tactics, and unique communication language designed

to induce IT management prospects to listen to your value. Follow the steps in order.

2. Your SVP is weak. When we advise senior management teams on best practices of how to grow IT company revenues, we use a holistic approach by integrating sales, marketing, strategy, and financial management into one outbound revenue capture program. When building their SVPs for them, we often spend weeks crafting a unique, specialized SVP based on the client's value. Focus on creating a unique SVP. If your cold calling is ineffective— change your SVP.

3. Instead of selling the appointment, you are trying to sell your technology, software, or professional services. Cold calling is one step in a sequential IT sales process to generate sales. Selling IT is a premeditated process. When you jump steps trying to shorten your sales cycle, you actually lengthen your sales cycle.

So, follow the script and the steps in order, and you will be able to penetrate the no talk zone of management. The following script example is for an IT health care application company, but it can easily be adapted to other industries.

Nine-Step IT Sales Telemarketing Script

Step 1   **Provide a personal introduction:** *"Hello, this is Paul DiModica."*

Step 2   **Offer a professional courtesy:** *"Thanks for taking my call."*

Step 3   **Provide the SVP:** *"We are Revenue Per Bed Improvement Specialists for the health care industry."*

Step 4   **Position that you are at the right title level by saying their title:** *"We work with CEOs in the health care industry like you."*

Step 5   **Describe the pain your SVP fixes in more detail:** *"Through our programs and services, we help health care CEOs maximize patient revenues and reduce operation expenses through a prepackaged, copyrighted process."*

Step 6   **Name drop references:** *"Due to our unique successes, we have worked with other health care firms like yours, including companies like XXX, YYY, and ZZZ."*

Step 7   **Identify your company's name:** *"I am calling from ABC."*

Step 8   **Ask for a small amount of time:** *"Can you and I meet for 20 minutes to chat?"*

Step 9   **Confirm that you value the executive's time:** *"I know you're busy. I will not waste your time."*

Each one of these steps is important. It communicates who you are, what makes you and your firm different, why you are calling in general, and that you respect the executive's time. Use this format and you will get in to meet the decision maker and will be seen as a peer—not a vendor.

You will notice nowhere in the nine-step telemarketing program that we immediately tell the targeted prospects I am selling technology. Only you care that you are selling technology. You are not a technology salesperson—you are a strategic advisor who uses technology as a tool to drive business results.

Fortune 1000 Selling. If you are selling to C-level executives at Fortune 1000 companies, some telemarketing methods and sales training courses will ask you to probe the contact with open ended questions on the first phone call to determine the business opportunity.

Let's be honest. You are not going to cold call the senior vice president of operations of the nation's largest supermarket chain and begin by probing him or her on his or her business needs with questions. The VP is not going to tell you! The VP doesn't know who you are. That only happens in sales training books written 20 years ago by people who don't sell technology and probably have a doctoral degree in training. Remember, the fact is you have to earn the right to sell to management—you don't automatically have it just because your management team told you to go sell to that company.

Here is an example of another telemarketing script used to penetrate the C-level suite:

Good day. My name is Paul DiModica. Thank you for taking my call. My firm and I are Milestone Management Specialists for venture capital funded companies. We specialize in working with CEOs like you. We help senior management teams complete VC contract milestones and ratchets on time and on budget. Companies like XXX, YYY, and ZZZ

*all use our services (name drop your best
clients). I am calling from ABC.*

*I am calling to see if you and I can meet for 20
minutes to chat about our services and to see
if we can help you with your business launch. I
will not waste your time.*

Telemarketing Do's and Don'ts

1. When telemarketing to senior executives, **never sell technology** on the phone. The only thing you are looking to do is **sell a 20-minute appointment**. This appointment can be in person or another conference call at a later date. But never explain what you do in detail on the phone; you are marketing results, not technology. Your entire communication time on the phone with the executive should **ideally be five minutes**, but **no longer than eight or nine minutes**, including the time to schedule an appointment at a later date.

2. If the executive starts asking you detailed questions about your service or application, push back and say, *"It is much more detailed than I can give you in five minutes on the phone. Let's set up a time to chat so I can explain in person. I will not waste your time."*

3. Be confident. Don't be wimpy. Executives are very busy. They will speak to you if you are confident and can help them be more successful in their jobs. Lack of confidence in what you say or what you sell can't be hidden. Prospects can sense fear like a dog.

4. When writing a technology sales telemarketing script, always include the line *"We specialize in [INSERT YOUR SVP], and we work with [INSERT TITLE OF PERSON YOU ARE SPEAKING TO]."* The reason for this is it proves to the gatekeepers as well as to your prospect that you are speaking with an executive with the appropriate management level and title (e.g., *"We work with CFOs." "We work with vice presidents of operations." "We work with presidents of small companies."*).

5. <u>Add value to your prospects</u>. You are there to help them be more successful. You are not calling them about the next big football game, or the weather, or the economy. You are calling them to <u>fix their business pain with your technology as the tool</u>. This pain could be lack of revenue, an expensive HR system, a website that has bad navigation or does not generate leads, or a boss who is angry with them because the competitors are taking away their market share.

6. One of the biggest mistakes most IT salespeople make is they do not plan their actions. Do not say *"Well, I guess I will call Paul today because I haven't spoken with him in three weeks."* Instead, plot why you are calling Paul and what your goal is when you talk to him. ***Always have a goal.*** To increase your IT sales cold calling success, schedule in your appointment book times to cold call, just like you schedule meetings. This way, you will treat cold calling like an important action step—instead of an afterthought.

Telemarketing to Fortune 1000 Companies

1. Cold call the C-level executive (CEO, CFO, CIO, etc.).

2. Talk with the executive for eight minutes or less to develop interest or direction.

3. Set up a 20-minute appointment either on site or via phone conference.

4. Meet for 20 minutes, validate why you should be there, and mine for opportunities. Before you leave, schedule another appointment.

5. Set up a new one-hour appointment to focus on opportunities/proposals.

6. Request to present to as many decision makers as dictated by the executive.

Depending on how your sales territory is set up (national, vertical, or local), you may be cold calling to set up your first appointment as a conference call. Just like an on-site appointment, you should schedule a follow-up appointment to talk for 20 minutes (only) to discuss your SVP.

Case History – Fortune 1000 Telemarketing Script

Below is another example of a script I put together to sell software. I worked with a company that sold Balanced Scorecard software and consulting services. The Balanced Scorecard is a Fortune 1000 strategy and measurement process used by senior executive teams. The software company was having a hard time reaching senior executives because the CIOs didn't understand the technology and the

CFOs kept pushing the salespeople back to the CIOs because the company was selling software.

So, I developed the following telemarketing script for the software company:

Good day. My name is Paul DiModica. Thank you for taking my call. We are specialists in the CFO Balanced Scorecard (or CIO Scorecard), and I am calling you to see if we can chat about potentially using a scorecarding methodology in your firm to increase corporate profitability. Companies like XXX use our services. I am calling from XYZ.

The Balanced Scorecard is known as a profitability tool by Global 1000 companies.

Immediately, this company's ability to get past the gatekeepers and reach the CFO increased dramatically.

Once when I was testing the script, I had an executive secretary say, *"Well I don't think he is the right person since this is software."*

I responded, *"Yes, he is the right person. He is the CFO, correct?"* When she responded with a yes, I then said, *"Well, this is the CFO Scorecard, and we only work with CFOs."*

She immediately transferred me to her boss. Don't let gatekeepers intimidate you. You are just doing your job.

Always ask for a 20-minute appointment **only**. This way, the executive will feel like he or she is in control when you meet (or chat again). Remember, it is important to be confident, but subservient to the executive's ego, so you can get the appointment. Arrogance never works with executives.

Always say you want to **chat**. It is a passive request to meet, and it will lower the walls of protection that automatically rise when an executive speaks with salespeople.

Have your talking points and objection responses handy when you start to cold call. Always be prepared. <u>Never shoot from the hip</u>.

Telemarketing to Small Businesses

1. Cold call the president.

2. Talk with him or her for only six to eight minutes to develop interest for an appointment.

3. Focus on how you will increase profits, decrease expenses, or manage business risks.

4. Set up a 20-minute appointment either on site or via phone conference.

5. Meet for 20 minutes, validate why you should be there, and mine for opportunities. Before you leave, schedule another appointment.

6. Develop a proposal, deliver it in person, and close the deal.

 TIP Any technology deal under $30,000.00 should take no more than two on-site appointments to close, and once you develop a scalable sales process you can replicate, this technology should be sold over the phone and through electronic online presentations.

Case History – Telemarketing Script for Web Design and Database Company

Here is another example of a script I put together for a web design company targeting small businesses:

Hello. My name is Paul DiModica. Thank you for taking my call. We are Business Development Specialists for accounting firms like yours, and we work with CEOs and senior partners like you to help them develop and implement professional communication programs to increase revenues. We have worked with other accounting firms like yours, including companies X, Y, and Z. I am calling from Value Forward Marketing.

I am calling to see if you and I can meet for 20 minutes to chat about our services and some of your firm's needs. I will not waste your time, and I will discuss with you how we can increase your company's revenue.

Cold Calling Small Businesses to Sell IT

If you are selling IT up and down the street to small businesses and not high rise buildings with security and are calling on firms that have fewer than 20 employees, get in your car and drive around. Walk into each office and ask for the owner.

Be friendly. Many times the employees are related. If the secretary asks why you are there, tell him or her you are just in the area and you want to introduce yourself to the owner for five minutes. If the secretary does not go get the owner or call to see if he or she is available, ask if you can set up a 20-minute appointment.

If the owner is not available and the secretary will not set up an appointment, leave some information and call back later.

If the owner comes out, say you were in the area and ask if he or she has five minutes to chat. After five minutes, set up an appointment, say thank you, and be on your way.

Cold calling in person still works in some markets—especially rural markets. In large cities, it's hard to cold call office by office due to security access and geography issues.

Accepting that no one likes to cold call means it must be hard to do. Riding a bike was hard to do in the beginning as well. After you practice and get the hang of it (and the success of it), you will see its value and will use it as part of your selling technology arsenal.

Small Business Sales

I have sold 8-figure IT deals and smaller deals to "mom and pop" businesses. A key question you need to ask is, what is your time worth? My experience selling professional services, enterprise applications, website development, and SaaS applications to small businesses is that you have to determine *how small* to go. I have found that small businesses with fewer than 10 employees are usually higher maintenance IT sales. The management team usually consists primarily of the owner, and budgets are so tight that owners will extend your selling cycle as they try to wheel and deal with your proposal price. Since your time is valuable, you may want to focus on a minimum price point, such as $3,000.00 or $5,000.00, as an entry point, even if you are selling by telephone or webinars. When selling any IT service or application offering valued at under $25,000.00, you should always try to sell long distance through interactive webinars, videos, and web proposals. The high cost of IT sales usually does not justify three to five on-site meetings with a prospect who may buy from you only 25 percent of the time.

Of course, there are exceptions to everything, and well-managed businesses with a professional management team or a venture capital funded start-up with only three employees may still buy $200,000.00 of technology or professional services from you. This is usually the exception instead of the rule when you get below that magic line of demarcation of 10 employees.

My recommendation to anyone selling technology, telecommunications, professional services, or software to the small business market is to focus on firms with 10 or more employees and you will increase your sales quota success. Time is money in IT sales.

Gatekeepers

When trying to sell senior executives of both small and large companies, you will invariably encounter the company gatekeeper. In small companies, this may be the receptionist. In large firms, this is usually an executive assistant who is responsible for keeping out people like you and me. But you can, and will, get past most them by using the following methods.

- When cold calling a large company, one method to get past the gatekeeper is to introduce yourself to him or her and treat this person as if he or she were the executive. Give the gatekeeper the courtesy of explaining what you do, and then ask if he or she can assist you in setting up a 20-minute phone conference with the boss. ***This is called the Friend Method.***

- If the gatekeeper will not help you and tries to pawn you off to some other executive, say politely, but confidently, *"Our firm only works with [INSERT EXECUTIVE'S TITLE], and our customers include XXX, YYY, and ZZZ. I appreciate your direction, but Mr./Ms. [INSERT EXECUTIVE'S NAME] is the right person I need to speak with."* ***This is called the Intimidator Method.***

- If you are trying to reach a C-level executive and you can't get a response, study his or her bio on LinkedIn or on the company's website. Find out what college the executive attended and send him or her a college hat or a team mascot figurine. Comment on the executive's alma mater's sports or academic success and then ask for a 20-minute meeting. ***This is called the I Am a Fan Method.***

- If the gatekeeper asks you for more detail on what you do (so he or she can make a judgment call for the boss), speak firmly, lower your voice, and say, *"I apologize. I do not mean to be rude, but my company only works with [INSERT EXECUTIVE'S TITLE]. Do you personally make these kinds of decisions? If not, then I would like to speak with Mr./Ms. [INSERT EXECUTIVE'S NAME]."* ***This is called the You're Only-a-Secretary Method. Warning: This is a last resort tactic that can backfire, so be cautious.***

- When a gatekeeper says, *"Please send your information, and Mr./Ms. XXX will follow up if he/she is interested,"* respond as follows: *"Ms. YYY, we specialize in [INSERT YOUR SVP], and many of our relationships with [INSERT EXECUTIVE'S TITLE] are personalized based on their corporate needs. I would like to send you some general information and then call you back next Tuesday to see if this meets Mr./Ms. XXX's needs and warrants a 20-minute conversation."* ***This is called the Pain Reliever Method.***

- If you consistently reach the executive's voice mail, prepare a voice mail script for yourself. Using a voice mail telemarketing script based on your SVP works great. I have had IT sales account executives get over 40 percent returned calls from C-level executives who were left a cold call message. Why? Because this method leaves an intriguing value proposition on the voice mail. The executive wants to know more and calls back. ***This is called the Voice Mail Method.***

* * *

Q: How often should you call?

A: That is a decision you will have to make based on your business opportunity costs. I have called a prospect 10 times in one day (without leaving messages) to set up an appointment in order to close a deal, and once a week for 47 weeks to present a seven-figure opportunity. If you call multiple times in one week, **never leave more than one voice mail message per week**. More than that and the prospect will think you are a pest. Multiple studies show the average salesperson usually gets through to the prospect between the fifth and the seventh call. So, be

persistent—and polite. It may be your job to keep
calling, but don't be obnoxious.

* * *

Objection Management Equals Appointments

No matter how good your script is, you are going to get
objections. In fact, you want the executive to ask you
questions because that means you have his or her attention.

The key is to sell the appointment, not the IT product or
service. To do this you need to walk a fine line between
giving basic information and offering complete disclosure of
why you are calling. You want to intrigue your prospects
with the concept of relieving their pain and making their
department or business more successful.

Remember: You don't sell technology and services—you sell
business results.

Telemarketing objections lead to appointments. So, you need
to create your script ahead of time—and practice.

Below are several objections I have gotten, along with the
responses I developed for previous SVPs. These are actual
objection scripts that have been successful.

Objection No. 1:

*What do you mean, you are Milestone Management
Specialists?*

Response:

> *What we do is help senior management teams like
> yours review and plot out strategic steps to implement
> their contractual milestones based on their VC
> contracts. What I would like to do is meet with you for
> 20 minutes to chat about our services.*

You will notice I gave the executive a little more information
than before, but not enough for him to make a decision on the
phone.

Objection No. 2:

> *How do you do this?*

Response:

> *What we do is review your business plan with you
> after we sign a nondisclosure agreement and then
> evaluate your needs as an executive to see how we
> can help you manage the VC ratchets. It will take
> about 20 minutes. Can we get together to chat? I will
> not waste your time.*

Again, a little more information, and then I closed for the
appointment.

This company was selling staffing professional services,
technology project work, business development consulting,
and web development. The CEO could not tell by my SVP
what I was really selling, and it interested him. But when you
look at venture capitalist contracts for dot coms (the target
market in this situation), the ratchets and milestones are
usually tied to having a website done by a certain date, hiring
"x" number of .NET programmers, and launching the

business development on time. So, my SVP actually matched my firm's technology services, but I had positioned us correctly to appeal to the CEO and his pain. By finding his pain, I bypassed the CIO, the vice president of human resources, and the vice president of operations, who might normally deal with my firm for our services (and all my competitors' services).

By finding this CEO's pain, I became a "doctor" and was allowed to make a "house call" (the appointment).

Objection No. 3:

Just send me some information. I am busy.

Response:

Yes, Mr./Ms. CEO, I know you are busy. It will only take 20 minutes, and companies like XXX, YYY, and ZZZ were also busy, but after spending 20 minutes with us, they decided we could help and became our clients—there must be a reason. Can you give me 20 minutes? I will not waste your time.

Objection No. 4:

I am not interested.

Response:

Ask why, and then wait for an answer and respond:

I am surprised, Mr./Ms. CEO, since we have worked with other companies like yours, including XXX, YYY, and ZZZ, and have helped them with their milestones. I would think you would be open to new business

*concepts that would increase your corporate profits
and increase your business valuation.*

Why are you not interested?

Follow-up comment:

*Is it acceptable for me to send you some information
and then to follow up in a week or two to see if you
may have reconsidered?*

If you get "I am not interested" more than 50 percent
of the time, then you need to review your SVP. The
key of an SVP is to intrigue executives with an
unusual interest in your concept, which they have
not heard about before.

Be creative. Invent.

Technology Sales Lead Generation

Although cold calling is the quickest way to build your
technology sales pipeline, other methods of prospecting
contacts will open doors for you as well. When combined
with technology cold calling, your lead generation will
prosper.

Method 1 - Direct Mail

Sending traditional direct mail (letters and response cards) to
the C-level executives of a Fortune 1000 company is usually
a waste of time and money. On a daily basis they are
inundated with junk mail from other B2B companies trying to
sell them on some new opportunity. (Think about how much

junk mail you get.) Usually they have executive assistants sifting through their mail, so the executives will not even see it. If your marketing department wants to spend its budget on this type of program to convince your management team the marketing directors are busy, then that's fine. But proportionately, the interest percentage will be small.

* * *

Q: So, how do you get to those Fortune 1000 executives?

A: The key is to be focused in your attack, using your SVP to get their attention.

* * *

The most successful direct mail method to set up a C-level executive appointment is to send executives a book with an inscription including your SVP and requesting a chat with them about your SVP. This is called dimensional mail. The book needs to be the most current business best-seller release (in hopes the executive has not yet read it) on leadership, management, or business success strategies, and it should somehow tie in to your unique SVP. Inside the book, write *Dear Mr./Ms. Prospect, I read this book and I thought it was intriguing so I decided to send it to you. We are [insert your SVP]. Can you and I chat for 20 minutes?*

* * *

Q: Why a book?

A: Because:

1.   It is a lot more expensive than a direct sales letter, so the C-level executive will not get very many of them.

2.   It will arrive in a box, so it will be hard to miss.

3.   It will encourage the C-level executive to think about your SVP (included in your inscription).

4.   It will open the door for your call requesting an appointment.

5.   When you call, you can tell the gatekeepers you are the person who sent the book. They always remember and may pass you right to the executive. If a gatekeeper says it looks like a great book (and you get to speak to the C-level executive), send a copy to the gatekeeper (or hand deliver it to him or her when you meet the executive).

* * *

Q: Does it work?

A: **Yes.** Let me give you an example:

Several years ago, I was working with a regional technology services client that wanted to reach the vice presidents of operations of Fortune 1000 prospects quickly.

To launch the program, I created the company's SVP, developed supporting marketing materials to match the SVP's message, and then mailed out 100 books to the targeted senior executives.

The boxes were shipped three-day delivery, and on the fifth day, we followed up with a phone call. Within one week, we had seven appointments (7%) with vice presidents of operations. Within 30 days, we had 16 appointments (16%), and three of these 16 called us to schedule directly.

Did it work? Yes.

* * *

Q: Will the book program work with small companies whose employee base ranges from 10 to 100?

A: **Definitely.** Small company CEOs and C-level executives receive even less attention than Fortune 1000 executives. Getting a free $28.00 book from you will generate discussion and should open the door for an appointment.

* * *

Q: Is it expensive?

A: No, it isn't. If you have developed the right SVP, are targeting the right prospect, and are communicating a compelling story, that $30.00 investment could be worth thousands of dollars in business.

* * *

Method 2 - Postcards

Fortune 1000 Companies

It may be hard to believe, but postcards work well with C-level executives. They are fast to read, repetitive, visible without opening an envelope, and cheap to produce. When sending a postcard, it should be a larger size (6"x8") and should not be gloss coated. The gloss coating does not work well with the U.S. Postal Service's sorters.

The key to having your message read is to make it direct and straightforward, with as few words as possible. It needs to scream your SVP to the C-level executive.

Then, on the back of the postcard, list the basic benefits of your SVP and your telephone number. That's it. Send it every month. It will get noticed and will generate interest (maybe even a phone call), and it will provide a smoother introduction when you cold call and might make it a warm call.

Case History – IT BI Applications and Project Management Services Sold to C-Level Executives

I was working with a client that was selling business intelligence (BI) software projects to CFOs of $100 million plus, privately owned manufacturing companies. This company was struggling to reach its targeted prospects, so I developed a new strategy approach, changed its website and white paper messaging, trained the sales team, and created new IT packaged offerings with unique names and pricing to build a replicable and scalable companywide revenue capture process. Once this was completed, I developed a six-postcard direct mail series to be mailed each week, with a follow-up telephone call after the fourth, fifth, and sixth mailings.

The postcards were large (8"x11"), and on the front they had one dominant word set against a strong, solid background color. For example, one said FEAR in bright red letters in 40-point font set against a high gloss black background. The second said STRESS in black letters set against a red background. On the back of each postcard, we discussed how manufacturing CFOs must take control and analyze their production cost information now—or they would end up experiencing FEAR (or STRESS).

We mailed these postcards every week for six weeks to a targeted list of 500 CFOs, followed by a phone call in the fourth, fifth and sixth weeks. By the end of the series, the client had set up appointments with 33 CFOs for a .066 percent response.

From those 33 first meetings, the sales team ended up selling $1.7 million in BI applications and projects during the next 12 months and developed a pipeline of new business for $9 million.

Do targeted postcards with the right SVP to C-level executives work? **<u>Yes!</u>**

Small Businesses Sales

Do postcards with your SVP on the front work for small businesses, too? Yes. Small business owners are more likely to read their own mail, which means your postcard is more likely to reach the president or owner.

Method 3 - Executive Seminars

Executive seminars and webinars work very well with Fortune 1000 companies and with small businesses.

Executive seminars are an effective way to generate leads for technology salespeople. But I <u>disagree</u> with the standard method most companies use for their production. Usually the marketing department comes up with a singular subject matter theme and then reproduces it on a regional basis to help the sales force. The problem with this method is that it does not build rapport and prospect interaction for the sales team. It is a shotgun approach that generates some leads but keeps moving as a "traveling road show." It is easy for the marketing department, but it reduces the seminar's overall effectiveness.

The most effective lead generating seminar approach is to package a **series of four seminars** in a particular geographic region, presented every month for four consecutive months. The subject matter needs to be relevant to C-level executives, and the event must be <u>by invitation only</u>. By having a series of seminars, you have the opportunity to bring back the same executives, as well as their peers, and to establish your firm as a source of knowledge.

Also, by packaging the four seminars together as a series for C-level executives, it allows you to sell sponsorships to noncompetitive partners to help support your marketing expenses. By keeping it <u>by invitation only</u>, you exclude unwanted competitors who are only trolling for contacts.

Theme. The key to reaching C-level executives is the subliminal sell. Your seminar themes should be based on important business success issues facing them in their daily business cycles and should be related to how YOUR SVP can fix their pain.

If you are selling ERP, CRM, or web development, *do not* have a seminar on these subjects. Don't do technology demos at these events. The C-level executives will not come. Have seminars like "How Hospitality CFOs Can Increase Profits in a Recession" or "How Manufacturing VPs Can Reduce Labor Costs During the Next 12 Months".

Speakers. <u>Never have your firm's management team be the speakers</u>. Your marketing department will push to have your team represented since it is paying for the events, but this is a mistake. This is just ego reinforcement for your management team. Your firm is to be the event's **<u>host only</u>**. Schedule executives from other noncompeting companies to be your speakers. Your seminar will appear to be a true educational seminar. Since it is your seminar, always have the speakers submit their presentations ahead of time to make sure they are succinct and to the point. Have the speakers market your seminar program to their own databases, but again, only to C-level executives. Try to coordinate your marketing with the speakers' marketing departments. Make sure the speakers are presenting generic, educational information at the seminar, not directly selling. **The way to get C-level executives to attend your seminar is to have C-level speakers.**

Sponsors. The nice thing about having a series of regionally based executive seminars (in the same city) is that you can have other firms sponsor the costs. The way to do this is to sell executive sponsorships. The sponsoring company will get the attendee's list after the presentation and will have its name on the advertising, mailing, and signage. It is similar to a golf tournament sponsorship. You get to meet and mingle under the entertainment tent for the price of an advertisement. Sponsors will usually volunteer to speak, so make sure they are the right fit. If you sell sponsorships, you can sell them individually for each seminar or as a package for the complete series.

Marketing. Having held multiple executive seminars and having managed marketing departments responsible for their implementation, I have come to the conclusion that the best method to generate attendance is the following (in descending order):

1. Mailed invitations (like a wedding invitation)

2. Opt-in email

3. Speakers' prospects mailing lists

4. Press releases/media

5. Print advertising

Your seminar series should be marketed at least **two months prior** to the first seminar's date. All invitations need to include an RSVP. All RSVPs should be confirmed with a follow-up letter, a seminar schedule, and the speakers' biographies. One week before each seminar's date, reconfirm all RSVPs with another letter (or by email). Confirm with the Chamber of Commerce or local publications that you have no competing organizations, sports events, or civic functions happening simultaneously on your scheduled seminar dates. You should shoot for a 10 percent attendance based on your mailing list. You can reach this target if you have a compelling reason for executives to attend the seminar, with

C-level speakers giving advice and information on industry trends.

Setup. I have found that Tuesday and Wednesday are the best days for executive technology seminars. There is big debate on what time your seminar should be held. Some say breakfast meetings, others say during the day, and still others say 6 p.m. to 8 p.m.

I have held the most successful C-level seminars from 6 p.m. to 8 p.m., and have served finger food.

Below is the format I have used successfully:

6 p.m. - 6:30 p.m.	Social Time/Food Served
6:30 p.m.	Seminar Begins (I ring a bell, like a theater bell, signaling the seminar is about to start.)
6:30 p.m. - 6:45 p.m.	Host and Speaker Biographies and Introductions
6:45 p.m. - 8 p.m.	Speaker Round Table Discussions/Audience Questions

Below is the process that has helped me to execute my seminars smoothly:

Before the Seminar

1. No more than three speakers are scheduled for the panel.

2. The panel submits questions ahead of time that are relevant to the seminar's subject matter focus.

3. All the potential questions are sent back to the panel to advise them of the questions that may be asked.

During the Seminar

4. Support staff is seated at a table at the entrance of the seminar's location to sign in invited guests and to hand out preprinted badges. Business cards are collected in a fish bowl.

5. A handout describes the hosting company, the sponsors, and the speakers' biographies, as well as the panel discussion format.

6. A table at the entrance (near the food) holds the sponsors' and host company's marketing materials.

7. When the seminar starts, the host stands at a lectern on stage or in front of the audience.

8. The host introduces him or herself, the sponsors, the host company and its SVP, and the panel speakers.

9. During the introductions, the host reminds the audience of the next scheduled seminar date and the subject matter to be discussed.

10. The panel is seated at a long table on stage with bottles/glasses of water.

11. Two standing microphones are placed in the audience to allow the audience's participation for questioning.

12. The host presents questions to the panel, and the panel responds.

13. PowerPoint is used only for panel introductions and for brief subject matter review. (PowerPoint presentations with a panel talking freely can be distracting to the audience.)

14. At the end of the discussion, the host thanks everyone for coming and reminds them of the next seminar date.

Case History – Executive Thought Leadership Seminar

I had a small technology client that was a start-up company and wanted to meet and sell to C-level management of Fortune 1000 prospects. We held a series of four monthly Executive Thought Leadership Seminars in one city by invitation only. Using the format described previously, we were able to sell executive marketing sponsorships for $200,000.00 to pay for the marketing (and more).

During the social time, the executive sponsor had its business development staff out in full force, shaking hands and getting introductions to all the C-level attendees.

The technology company averaged 140 people per seminar, with more than 90 percent being C-level executives. Since this was a start-up company, it launched its name, its brand,

and its revenue stream while someone else paid for the marketing.

For small business technology sales, this is a great way to dominate a regional geography. By partnering with other small business suppliers and service providers like accountants, lawyers, and consultants, you can easily cover the cost of your seminars and marketing while developing new customers and prospects for all.

Thought Leadership Webinars

Like Thought Leadership Seminars, Thought Leadership Webinars are another business success tool you should use to create inbound leads and corporate positioning.

Method 4 - Touch Management (Passive)

Selling technology is a sport. It requires you to train and constantly prepare for your time on the field. One of the key ways to sell technology successfully is to have your firm's name in front of the executive decision makers on a regular basis. To play, you have to be invited to the game. The way to do this is by an automated touch program, continually sending marketing messages to your target market on a regular basis.

This may include postcards, press releases, direct sales letters, marketing collateral, and client testimonials. Once a month, you need to touch the prospect. Technology-buying clients generally have their own buying cycles, which, in most cases, do not parallel your selling cycle. So, by keeping you firm's name in front of buyers on a repetitive basis, you have a better chance of having them contact you when they are ready. This is a **passive** process of lead generation, so set it up with your marketing department or an outside firm (or do it yourself), and then forget about it.

Method 5 - Network Management/Spiff Management

If you are seeking to increase your lead generation, one of the quickest ways is through any and all strategic partners you currently have. This works both with small businesses and with Fortune 1000 companies.

Fortune 1000 Companies

Partnering with the individual channel representatives of your company's current strategic partners (in your local territory) takes time, an expense account, and mutual lead sharing. The key with local partner reps is to spend time with them. Most channel partner managers have multiple relationships in a specific geography, so they have many options when it comes to whom they send their leads. The more they get to know you, the more apt they will be to share leads with you.

Other areas of networking include:

- Chamber of Commerce business meetings

- Local technology groups' monthly meetings (TIE, WIT, TAG, etc.)

- Local technology magazines' meet and greet meetings

Small Businesses

If you sell to small businesses consisting of more than 10 employees, you have a great opportunity for a tremendous amount of leads through local partnerships. These partnerships will not happen unless you get out and introduce yourself. When appropriate, offer a 10 percent finder's fee (based on collection) to anyone who introduces you to a prospect that generates revenue.

Just imagine how many small business leads you might have depending on the technology you sell if you partnered with just two members in each of the following categories:

1. Accountants

2. Lawyers

3. Business insurance agents

4. Chambers of Commerce

5. Local lead clubs

6. Local Toastmasters clubs

7. Local computer hardware companies

8. Other software companies (those you do not compete against)

9. Business consultants

10. Local college professors (especially community colleges)

11. Business real estate agents

12. Local church groups

13. Local advertising firms

14.   Local printers

These selected groups are involved in the community on a daily basis. They know which businesses are growing, which ones are adding staff, which companies are seeking services, and the name of each president or key contact. If you partner with just two contacts in each of these categories, you will have more leads than you can handle. Meet with them personally, explain what your firm does, show examples of your work if appropriate, and then put them on your mailing list. Buy them lunch and spread the word.

The IT Sales Success Secret Formula

Sales Value Proposition + Senior Level Executives + Transaction Selling Techniques + Discuss Pain x 20 Cold Calls a Day = Dramatically Increased IT Sales!

The secret formula to IT sales success in today's economy is specific actions linked to sequential steps. It requires practice, persistence, and confidence in your delivery approach that you are a peer—not a vendor—when communicating your value to qualified prospects.

1.   Create the right SVP.

2.   Work only with higher level titled executives and build trust.

3. Understand that relationships don't start until the second IT sale, and force your prospects to take action steps with you during the sales cycle.

4. Always focus on how your IT offering helps the prospect's business become more successful.

5. Make the prospect take a transactional step to prove to you they are qualified.

6. Manage your time.

7. Make at least 20 new cold calls a day to new prospects.

Highlights of this section:

- Sell up, never down.

- Acquiring technology today is now a boardroom decision.

- Go for the heavy hitters, and you will become a heavy hitter.

- If you call before 8 a.m. or after 5:30 p.m., you are likely to reach a C-level executive instead of his or her assistant.

- Cold call in-person those companies with fewer than 20 employees. Set up an appointment if possible.

- Determine how small is too small.

- Determine your minimum price point.

- When cold calling, never sell technology over the phone. Always set up a 20-minute appointment.

- Be confident. Executives respect confident people.

- When writing your telemarketing script, include your SVP, identify the title-type to whom you are speaking, and add value to your prospect (e.g., *"We specialize in [INSERT YOUR SVP] and are working with [INSERT EXECUTIVE'S TITLE] to relieve [INSERT EXECUTIVE'S PAIN]"*).

- Plan your actions and always have a goal.

- Do not let the gatekeepers intimidate you.

- Always say you want to chat.

- If you cold call multiple times in one week, never leave more than one voice mail message.

- Objection management equals appointments.

- Build your pipeline through lead generation.

Exercises:

1. Schedule time in your appointment book to cold call three times each week. Load at least 400 companies into your database.

2. Analyze a telemarketing script. Break it out with the following steps:

    Step 1   Provide a personal introduction: *"Hello. This is [INSERT YOUR NAME]."*

    Step 2   Offer a professional courtesy: *"Thanks for taking my call."*

Step 3   Provide the SVP: *"We are [INSERT YOUR SVP] Specialists."*

Step 4   Position that you are speaking with the right title level: *"We work with [INSERT EXECUTIVE'S TITLE] like you."*

Step 5   Describe the pain your SVP fixes: *"Through our programs and services, we help you ...[INSERT THE VALUE OF YOUR OFFERING."*

Step 6   Name drop references: *"Companies like XXX, YYY, and ZZZ."*

Step 7   Identify your company's name: *"I am calling from [INSERT YOUR COMPANY]."*

Step 8   Ask for a small amount of time: *"Can we meet for 20 minutes?"*

Step 9   Confirm that you value the executive's time: *" I know you're busy. I will not waste your time."*

3.   Develop talking points and objection responses. Keep them handy.

4.   Develop a voice mail script.

5.   Send a book to 10 of the C-level executives you would like to reach.

Chapter

4

The First Meeting:
Presenting to Prospects

After reading this chapter, you will learn:

- How to handle the 20-minute appointment

- How to present your SVP so the C-level executive will see you again

- How to present your technology to a C-level executive

- How to develop a technology team talking points document script

- How to mine for business opportunities

When setting up their first IT prospect meetings, many technology salespeople believe they need to become experts in their prospects' needs by over researching their backgrounds through their websites, press releases, annual reports, and company brochures.

This is totally wrong.

Why?

Because when you over research a prospect BEFORE you speak with him or her, you develop a preconceived perception of what you think is the business pain this person is prepared to admit he or she needs to pay to have fixed.

Yet many salespeople still believe that having specific knowledge about a prospect company at the first meeting is the key to increasing sales closing success.

Sell More IT—By Doing Less Prospect Research

Selling IT is not about you (and how educated you are) … it's about buyers, so you have to get them to admit openly to their business pain for them to fund its repair. If a prospect will not admit to a business pain—that company will never pay to fix it. So, don't focus on a buyer's specific business problem background before the first meeting; instead, study the industry's unique business pains to position yourself as an industry specialist about the industry—not about your prospect's business problems specifically. *It's not the pitch. It's the business pain they admit!*

How to Become an Industry Expert in 5 Minutes or Less

As mentioned before, the fastest way to become an industry expert in any business vertical is to go to the trade association website of that industry (National Restaurant Association, National Manufacturing Association, etc.), print out 5 to 10 pages of the home page and associated information web pages, and then circle the words you do not understand. Look up the words on Google, and now you will know the language of that industry. Then go back to the website and print out the association's annual trade show brochure. Read the names of the trade show breakout sessions and workshops—these are the business problems of that industry. Use this approach to prepare for your 20-minute meeting.

The First 20-Minute Appointment

So, you have cold called your C-level executive or small business president, and now you have a 20-minute appointment.

* * *

Q: Why 20 minutes?

A: The key to dealing with executives is understanding they value their time more than you do. You are an IT salesperson. There are tens of thousands of account managers like you floating around in the market.

Prospects get calls from people like you all the time. For you to get the appointment just by using your unique SVP is the exception to the rule.

* * *

By making the appointment for only 20 minutes, you have given the executive enough time to decide if you will add value or waste his or her time.

So, your goal in your 20-minute appointment is as follows:

1. Reintroduce your sales value proposition.

2. Validate to the executive that you have the right to be speaking with him or her and that you are a peer.

3. Communicate that you are an industry specialist.

4. Mine for business opportunities based on the business pains they admit to.

5. Qualify the prospect.

6. Set up your next sequential sales cycle step appointment, usually a 1-hour executive briefing.

That's it. You are not there to sell $650,000.00 of technology applications or professional services the first time you meet a prospect. You are not there to sell a $25,000.00 software accounting package. You are there to **prove you belong there** as a business peer and to mine for qualified opportunities.

If you try to sell now (at this early stage), you will not make it to 20 minutes.

Remember, selling technology and professional services is a premeditated process—jumping your sales steps will just elongate your sales cycle.

Your SVP is what got you in the door. Staying there is based on your skill sets as a salesperson and on your preparation.

Twenty Minutes and Counting

The goal of your 20-minute meeting is to qualify the prospect and either take him or her to the next sales cycle action step or put him or her into a passive marketing mode, contacting this person once a month until he or she moves into a buying cycle.

Remember, the buying cycle and the selling cycle are always different, so you need to manage the timeline between these two until they meet. Trying to sell professional lookers or qualified prospects that have not yet entered into the buying cycle is a waste of time, and it reduces your potential to hit your IT sales quota and to increase your income.

Four Steps of Your First 20-Minute Meeting

There are four steps in your first 20-minute meeting. Each step is sequential and has a symbiotic relationship with the preceding step.

Each step should take approximately **5 minutes**.

Step 1 – Introductions

- Re-communicate your SVP to the targeted prospect.

- Tell your prospect about your company's history.

- Tell how your IT offering can help your prospect's company increase income, decrease expenses, manage business risks, or improve agility.

- Tell your prospect the clients with which you have worked.

Pitch

Thank the C-level executive for seeing you, hand your business card to him or her, and then sit down and say:

Mr./Ms. Smith, I know you are busy, so let me follow up on what we chatted about on the phone. Our firm specializes in [STATE YOUR SVP]. We have been in business X years, and we work with other clients like you in the [INSERT XX INDUSTRY] to help them increase corporate income (decrease expenses, or manage business risks) using our technology as business tools that drive results.

My firm has worked with other executives in the XXX industry like you, including XXX, YYY, and ZZZ.

Step 2 – The Bridge Step

- Validate that you have a reason to be there.

- Describe to your prospect the top five to seven business problems that are common in their market which you discovered from their vertical industry association websites to position yourself as a specialist.

The goal of the second step is to communicate to the executive that you are a business peer, not a vendor, and that you are an industry specialist. Step 2 is called the bridge step because it allows the targeted prospect to validate that you are an equal. It also helps the prospect to identify intellectually that the problems his or her company has are the same business problems his or her industry peers have. Once a prospect accepts that his or her business issues are common, more often than not, he or she will then that admit his or her company has business pains your technology may be able to fix—bridging you to the third step in your 20-minute meeting.

Pitch

In your second step, say the following:

We work with CEOs, CFOs [STATE EXECUTIVE'S TITLE], and companies like XXX, YYY, and ZZZ, helping them increase revenues (or reduce expenses).

Recently, CIO magazine [NAME A THIRD PARTY REFERENCE] said there are five main business events affecting companies like yours in the manufacturing [NAME THE BUSINESS VERTICAL] industry. They include [LIST THE FIVE EVENTS].

I am just curious; is your firm experiencing any of these same common events?

Now wait for the prospect to respond. If you have done your industry research correctly, statistically the IT prospect will be experiencing at least one of the five to seven events (issues) currently affecting his or her peers.

Make sure the business problems that are common in the buyer's industry can be fixed by your IT offering.

Step 3 – Mining for Sales Opportunities

So far, you have set up your IT business value, positioned your firm as a specialist, and opened the door for the targeted buyer to admit to having business problems common in their industry.

But we do not know if the prospect is qualified.

So, let's wait and see how the prospect responds to your Step 2 question: *"I am just curious; is your firm experiencing any of these same common events?"*

Now wait for an answer.

If the C-level executive starts talking about business problems his or her company is having, start taking notes because that is what you are going to sell them on.

When the executive is finished, respond that your IT offering is a business success tool designed to help fix or eliminate the problem(s) your prospect has just admitted to.

Explain what you do in more detail, but don't describe what you sell. Instead, describe the outcomes, benefits, and business results your IT offering produces. Remember, C-level executives (in B2B companies big and small) care about **only** four things: **reducing expenses**, **increasing revenue**, **managing business risks and/or consequences**, or **improving agility**.

Use the right words to communicate value:

Wrong Verbiage	**Right Verbiage**
We sell web applications.	We work with clients like you to increase digital revenue through automation.
We place technology candidates.	We help you reduce your human capital costs and maximize your business operational efficiencies.
We offer a unique CRM system that has been highly reviewed by independent research firms.	Our client capture success programs increase your sales team's closing ratio while reducing your marketing costs.

At this point you have communicated your value and identified that the prospect has a need for the type of IT or professional services you sell. But you have not yet identified if the prospect is a qualified buyer. This is the difference between being a great IT salesperson or an average salesperson. Just because a prospect has a need for your IT offering does not mean he or she is qualified. The world is full of professional lookers who will waste your valuable selling time and steal your commissions.

In Step 3, if the prospect admits to a business problem common to the industry that your IT offering can fix, before you can proceed to Step 4 in your 20-minute meeting, you must qualify the prospect by asking specific, transactional selling questions.

These questions are to be asked randomly in a conversational tone, but their answers will dictate your next action step during your 20-minute meeting.

- *Mr./Ms. Prospect, do you have a budget or funding to fix this area in your company?*

- *If we move forward, who will be the person signing the agreement or the paperwork?*

- *If our offering is a good fit for your firm, when do you want to be operational?*

- *Who else on your team will be involved in making a decision to move forward?*

- *What benefits will your company generate if we are able to resolve these issues in your firm with our IT offerings?*

By asking these questions, you will be able to decide, based on the answers you receive, either to move forward in your sales process to Step 4 or to put this prospect into a passive marketing model, following up on a monthly basis as you wait for the prospect's buying cycle and your selling cycle to coincide.

Remember, transactional selling forces prospects to prove to you that they are qualified buyers.

Don't skip the all-important step of qualifying your prospect.

Why? Consider this:

- As a professional IT salesperson, do you want to start a sales cycle with someone who won't be buying your

type of IT offering until 18 months from today?
Remember, time management is a key driver of using
the 3T process of IT sales (Trust, Transactional, Time
Management).

- As a professional IT salesperson, do you want to start
  a sales cycle with someone who has no funding to buy
  your offering?

- As a professional IT salesperson, do you want to start
  your sales cycle with a prospect who does not sign
  contracts and who is going to become your value
  intermediary and your salesperson to the decision
  maker?

A prospect with a need is not enough. The key to being a
successful IT salesperson is this: You must work with
prospects who have the potential to buy within your normal
selling timeline and who move with you in tandem, taking
action steps in a forward momentum, proving to you they are
not wasting your time.

You don't get paid for proposals or demos or RFP
responses—only signed contracts.

If the prospect answers the questions in Step 3 correctly, then
move to Step 4 and ask him or her if you and your firm can
set up a more detailed, one-hour executive briefing
appointment with the rest of the executive management team.
During this meeting, you will discuss your SVP and how
your IT offering can help your prospect's company improve
its business results.

Remember, as an IT salesperson, you are a business success
coach.

If during Step 3 the prospect denies having any of the common industry business problems you discussed in Step 2, he or she is not telling the truth. It's just ego.

You can try asking open-ended questions to bring out your prospect's true issues. But remember, you have 20 minutes. So don't waste your time with someone who is in denial. If a senior level executive prospect will not admit that his or her company has a business problem, then that person will never find funding to fix the problem.

During your 20 minute meeting, ask prospects who deny having common industry problems open-ended questions like:

- **How come** your firm does not have any of these events going on?

- **How long ago** did you investigate these areas and decide not to make changes?

- **Why doesn't** your firm outsource?

- **When will you** consider an investment in this technology area?

But again, if you can't get the prospect to admit after 20 minutes that he or she needs your IT, then just thank him or her for spending time with you and say you will follow up in the future when events may change.

Then put this prospect into your passive marketing model and follow up (cold calls, direct mail, thought leadership events, etc.) every month until your prospect's buying cycle and your selling cycle intersect. If during your conversation, the prospect has a need but is not qualified, move them into a passive marketing model and move on.

Step 4 – Set Up Your Next Appointment

If after going through Step 3, the prospect openly admits to having business problems that are common in the industry and answers correctly your qualifying questions, then you proceed to Step 4 and set up your next appointment.

Based on the price of your IT offering and the type of technology or professional services you sell, your next appointment could be a long distance executive briefing or an on-site meeting. In either case, your next meeting should last no longer than one hour.

At this point you are NOT going to do an application demo or client specification development. Your next meeting should be an executive briefing. Even if your offering is under $25,000.00, doing a three-hour, bore me to tears feature/function presentation at this point in your sales cycle is only going to force you into commodity with the targeted buyer. There is plenty of time later to show how great your IT is—but first you must reconfirm your business value and get all the decision makers into one room to talk about their business problems in more detail. **Business case first, technology demo second.**

Engagement Outlines

To help solidify your business value and that you want a peer-to-peer relationship and not a peer-to-vendor relationship, at the end of Step 4 in your 20-minute meeting, hand the qualified prospect an engagement outline.

Engagement outlines are preprinted sequential step guidelines you want the buyer to take with you in tandem to help you manage the buying process. The key words here are *YOU are managing the buying process.*

Many sales training courses incorrectly teach IT salespeople to work with decision influencers as equals to help them close decision makers. But this is wrong. The way to manage decision influencers is through the decision maker's authority. One tool to accomplish this is the engagement outline.

To build your engagement outline:

1. Insert your company's name at the top.

2. Insert your company's logo at the top.

3. Insert your SVP at the top.

4. List in sequential order the action steps <u>you</u> want the buyer to take with you during your sales cycle.

When building out your sequential sales steps, make sure you have at least three follow-up executive meetings listed in your outline. By forcing repetitive executive meetings, you have a fallback position when you are delegated to lower-level decision influencers who want to take control of your sales cycle.

If you get subordinated to lower-level managers during your sales cycle timeline and they slow up your selling process, pull out your engagement outline and reconfirm with them the agreed-to engagement steps (buying steps) their

114

executives discussed with you during your first 2(
meeting.

To sell larger deals more effectively, always insert into youɪ
engagement outline that you want the buying executives to do
a tour of your corporate office, and offer to pay for it. What is
$5,000.00 in travel and entertainment costs when compared
to the prospect's lifetime value for a $100,000.00,
$200,000.00, $1,000,000.00, or more IT sale?

Engagement Outline Example

Client Engagement Outline	
Phase 1	Information Exchange
Phase 2	Executive Briefing—Business Needs Assessment
Phase 3	Executive Briefing—Business Discovery
Phase 4	Service or Product Presentation
Optional	Visit our office for a tour
Phase 5	Prospect Proposal Development
Phase 6	Executive Briefing—Proposal Delivery and Discussion
Phase 7	[YOUR COMPANY] Selected as a Preferred Vendor
Phase 8	Executive Briefing—Proposal and Contract Finalized
Phase 9	[YOUR COMPANY] Assigns Team Leader to Manage Product/Service Delivery

Client Engagement Outline. A list of steps expected during
the sales cycle.

At the end of Step 4 of your 20-minute meeting, pull out your
engagement outline and say:

> *Mr./Ms. Prospect, since we are specialists in*
> *[INSERT YOUR SVP], we have developed in*
> *tandem with our other client successes an*
> *engagement outline to use as a talking points*
> *document between us to determine if working*
> *together is a good fit.*

Then go through each step listed on the document, describing in detail for the executive the step's significance. Use this engagement outline to help manage your sales process to minimize roadblocks and requests that are out of cycle expectations.

Once you have presented your engagement outline and discussed it with the prospect, finish your 20-minute meeting and schedule a one-hour executive briefing.

If the executive says, *"Your (SVP) process sounds interesting; talk to my secretary, and have him or her set up an appointment with my VPs and me,"* as you leave the C-level executive's office, say hello to the secretary and inform him or her that the boss just said he or she needs to set up an appointment in the near future. Then ask the secretary (right there while you are standing in front of him or her) if he or she will check the executive's schedule to see when an appointment is possible.

If the C-level executive says, *"This is interesting. I want you to meet with John, my VP of delivery,"* ask the executive (while you are sitting in his or her office) if he or she will email John to let him know the executive would like the two of you to meet.

If the C-level executive doesn't walk you out to the main door, call John immediately from the lobby and say, *"Hi,*

John. My name is [INSERT YOUR NAME], and I just met with [INSERT C-LEVEL EXECUTIVE'S NAME]. We specialize in [STATE YOUR SVP], and [INSERT C-LEVEL EXECUTIVE'S NAME] wants me to meet with you."

In your 20-minute meeting, if after you give the C-level executive your SVP process and the speech about increasing the company's revenue and reducing expenses (or managing risks), he or she still says, *"I am not the right person,"* then ask, *"Can you direct me to the right person in the company?"*

If the executive tries to send you down lower in the organizational chart to a commodity level manager (below vice president in the United states), respond, *"I appreciate that direction, but we usually work with the executive management team first from a business model approach,"* and pull out your engagement outline to use as a talking points tool.

If the executive is persistent in directing you to lower-level managers, then call those contacts and tell them the C-level executive told you to call, start the process over again, and use your engagement outline as a commodity sales control tool with the next contact to whom you are directed.

* * *

Q: Why does this IT and professional services selling process work?

A: The current economy is dragging Fortune 1000 companies and business owners of privately held companies through a business paradigm shift. Today, it is not "Do I need technology," but instead it is "How do I survive and improve my operation—so tell me how your IT is a business tool that will accomplish this." If you communicate your value correctly, business decision makers will take an action step to buy and will find funding to buy.

* * *

In IT sales, three truisms apply to all prospect company sizes:

1. **Fear Has No Budgets.** So help your prospects three dimensionally feel the fear of what will happen to their companies (or departments) if they don't buy your IT or services, or if they buy from the wrong company.

2. **CEOs, Presidents, COOs, CFOs, and Business Owners Don't Have Budgets—Only Department Managers Do.** CEOs, C-level executives and business owners always get what they want—but they will find the money only if you can convince them of your offering's value—so focus high in organizational charts—not low.

3. **Price Must Equal Value.** If the prospect thinks your IT offering is too high priced, it is because you explained your value wrong.

The words used in your script should be specific to the executive's needs. When communicating your market differentiation with your firm's SVP (and SVP marketing materials), focus on these executive management team pressure points:

*   Increase corporate profits

- Reduce corporate expenses

- Integrate business department communication

- Specialists in ...

  o Performance management

  o Customer retention

  o Customer maintenance

- Improve customer lifetime value

- Key performance drivers

- Operational blueprint

- Reduce operational overhead

- Increase operational efficiencies

- Customer capture

- Client communication enhancement

Case History – The First Appointment

Using the previous method, I penetrated one of the largest hotel companies in the world. For two years, a company I worked for had been unable to sell professional technology services to this client in volume. I was the corporate vice president of strategy, and one of our divisional vice presidents of sales asked me to help.

Here is what I did:

1. I cold called the CFO and sent him a book.

2. I spoke with him on the phone and explained to him our unique SVP.

3. He said he was interested, but he was traveling for the next 30 days to hotel sites. He then directed me to call the CIO and set up an appointment for the both of them.

4. I called the CIO and told him the CFO requested that I meet with them. I also told him I would like to meet for 20 minutes, and I would not waste their time.

5. I sent them each a book and a copy of my marketing SVP brochures, and I met with them in the CFO's private office.

6. I introduced myself again, stated our SVP, explored the industry's pains, discussed why we were different, explained how we could fix those pains, and then mined opportunities.

The appointment's outcome:

The 20-minute appointment lasted 1½ hours. When I left, there were three other vendors waiting in the CFO's office for their late appointments. I left with three new separately scheduled one-hour appointments (that I had scheduled while I sat in the CFO's office) to discuss three business pains the firm was experiencing...as well as my IT offering.

Within six months, we became a preferred vendor with that client and were scheduled to generate in excess of $10 million in business over the next three years.

What were the technology services I was selling? Project work, web development, and IT staffing. Stuff that usually gets delegated to a director of development or a human resource manager.

But by developing an SVP that appealed to the C-level executives and discussing profit improvement and expense reduction, I was able to sell more conceptually and get the business.

Buyer Talking Points

One area where many experienced technology salespersons fail is in the preparation of a sales call. I remember, early in my career, going out with my vice president of sales and three development and operations types to present to a Fortune 50 company.

When I asked if we were going to have a pre-meeting to get ready for our technology demonstration, I was told by the (then) vice president of sales that he had been working with the client for over a year and that he was ready. Additionally, he said I should just listen and learn.

So, we all trooped out to the company's executive conference room, took our seats, and waited for the meeting to begin. Mr. VP of Sales set up his overhead presentation and our system's application demonstration and waited for the executive buying team to arrive.

As soon as the personal introductions were made, Mr. VP of Sales started into his sales pitch and went into his automated sales call process mode. He didn't stop talking for 45 minutes straight. Moving from the PowerPoint to our applications demo, he seemed smooth and knowledgeable. After 45 minutes, the clients started to ask questions, which Mr. VP responded to firmly and in detail. After 1½ hours, Mr. VP of Sales had completed his demonstration and asked if there were any additional questions.

The senior vice president of operations, who had sat through the entire software demonstration quietly, said no and thanked us very much for our time. When Mr. VP of Sales asked what would be the next step, we were informed the Fortune 50 management team would get back to us.

So, we packed up our bags and headed out to our rental car, threw our bags into the trunk, and raced to the airport to catch our flight home. As we headed down the highway at 90 miles an hour, Mr. VP of Sales said loudly from the back seat, *"How do you guys think it went? They seem pretty interested!"*

Well, of course, they weren't. Thirty days later we were told the Fortune 50 company had signed a Letter of Intent (LOI) with one of our competitors. They were currently working out the details of the contract. **A contract worth $13 million!**

Having worked with many technology clients in public, private, established, family-run, and start-up companies, I have seen this scenario over and over again. It is hard to believe, but experienced technology sales executives and senior management teams continually wing it when they are on a sales call—just going into sales on autopilot without any pre-sales call preparation. Salespeople spend a large amount of time prospecting, marketing, and positioning their company to meet and greet the right C-level decision maker, but then spend 5 minutes on what they are going to say, failing to prep for the big meeting.

When presenting to IT executive buyers, build buyer dictionaries and personalized presentations based on the social, economic, and demographic words and operating needs of the targeted buyers. Don't use an auto-selling process that treats everyone as if they were the same.

CFOs of privately held $100 million health care companies use different language to describe their business needs than CFOs of privately held $100 million manufacturing companies.

Focus on the buyer's needs (and language), not on your company's verbose technology-laden acronyms created by some vice president of operations or services who knows nothing about marketing and selling.

Managing Sales Objections

Sales objections should be viewed simply as your prospects communicating to you how you can sell more. Never fear sales objections because, if handled correctly, any good IT salesperson can use them as a strategic tool to move the sales process transactionally to the next sales step. The best way to manage sales objections is to develop a written, top 10 sales objection talking points document that helps you and your team give pre-developed, structured responses to the objections you anticipate hearing most. This top 10 sales objection document should include every objection that could slow down or stop your sales cycle's forward momentum.

These objections might be true or false (and even spread by your competitors), but it does not matter. If an objection is verbalized, then it must be managed because in sales, perception is reality. The sales objections most salespeople incorrectly manage are the silent sales objections: the ones the prospect has but does not articulate, or the ones the prospect is not smart enough to ask.

As stated earlier, buyers often don't know how to buy correctly, so letting them manage your sales commissions by counter punching you with off the cuff comments and questions you are not prepared for seems counterproductive. To increase your sales closing ratios, always proactively prepare for and handle both visible and invisible sales objections—before they happen—by educating target prospects on why they should buy from you.

Successful technology salespeople do not wing it.

Case History – A Second Appointment Gone Wrong

Recently, I sat through an appointment as a high tech business success coach with several senior level vice presidents of a Fortune 100 company with my client's sales vice president and his presentation team. My client had been in business for many years and had unusual technology this Fortune 100 company could quickly deploy. The sales VP had over 10 years of experience in sales and had been previously employed by one of the largest software companies in the world.

Prior to his current position, the sales VP had been exposed to multiple structured sales training courses on how to sell. Yet as I observed his presentation, it was amateur hour at the Apollo.

At the beginning of the meeting, the C-level contact informed everyone he had only one hour available for this presentation. So to hit the timeline, the sales VP immediately launched into his demo without supplying any company history or his SVP.

Mistake 1: Don't make them wonder who you are.

Mistake 2: Always provide an intriguing reason to draw them into the demo.

As the prospects started to ask questions about the vendor's history, another presenter in the room attempted to respond and was cut off by the sales VP, who bellowed that he would answer that question.

Mistake 3: Always work as a team.

I could feel the tension in the room between my client and the prospects.

Unfortunately, it got worse. During the software application presentation, the sales VP's demonstration screen locked up (as software sometimes does). He then started talking out loud, muttering, *"Something is wrong here; it's not working right."*

Mistake 4: Never let them see you sweat.

To prevent this type of embarrassment, follow the steps provided in this book and be a pro. Always prepare *typed* talking points and discussion topics for yourself and everyone involved.

Mistake 5: Don't assume IT buyers know how to buy your IT (regardless of their titles).

For your first 20-minute appointment, your talking points should include:

- Your introduction; who you are
- Your firm's background and your existing clients
- Your SVP and why your firm is different
- Your prospect's business description
- The pain your prospect's industry is experiencing
- How your SVP will fix this pain
- Your prospect's product or service needs (mine for opportunities)
- Transactional qualification questions
- Your request for a new appointment to discuss a specific opportunity

Communicating With the Executive

Well, you have made it to the boardroom or the inner office of the senior executive. Most technology salespeople don't make it this far, or they take too long in the sales cycle to get here. But you're here. So, let's not waste your time or the executive's time.

After you have communicated your company's history, discussed your SVP, and reviewed the industry's picture, you now want to dig deep into mining for buying opportunities.

Many sales training courses talk about asking open-ended questions to flush out the prospect's true needs and wants.

Forget it. Those sales approaches are **old school** and are designed for the little people in management, who have a tendency not to know all the facts, or for those who play games. You are now dealing with the top people, and the old system will not work.

This is a senior executive. Do not waste his or her time. The executive talks business and money all the time. Transactional selling is the key to more IT sales. Focus on getting prospects to prove to you they are qualified. To sell executives, be direct and tell them how your IT can make them more successful.

Transactional Selling Questions That You Can Use During the 20-Minute Meeting to Prove the Prospect Is a Qualified Buyer

You're a strategic advisor. Stop acting like a bits and bytes, speeds and feeds salesperson. I know your software applications are great, your executive management reports are unbelievable, your delivery is the best in the business, and you have been told many times by your executive team that your development staffers are gurus.

But who cares? Not the buyer. All that corporate gobbledygook will not help you make more money. All buyers care about is how your technology or professional service is going to increase income, reduce operating expenses, manage business risks, or improve business agility.

All you should care about is this: Am I selling to a qualified buyer or wasting my time with a professional looker?

So, now is the time. Lean forward and look the buyer right in the eye, and ask these **DIRECT** questions, using a conversational tone:

1. Do you have a budget for this project?
2. When will the decision be made?
3. Who will be making the decision with you?
4. What other companies are you speaking with?
5. If you decide to move forward, who will be signing our paperwork?
6. When do you want to be operational?
7. How do you see our IT offering helping your firm?

When working with senior executives, always ask direct questions.

Talking Points for Prospect Meetings

The sales process, by its very nature, requires repetitive tasks. Cold calling, sending out follow-up e-mails to prospects, developing proposals, and managing customer issues are all daily tasks required to hit and exceed your sales quota.

In consulting with many companies, it surprises me how often experienced salespeople do not plan their sales calls and fall into a repetitive presentation model based on previous experiences with "like" prospects. They just wing it because they are *senior* salespeople. **Do not autosell. Always prepare for each new twenty-minute meeting like it is your first sales opportunity.**

Do not wing this part. Professional salespeople do not shoot from the hip. The key to supporting your sales value proposition is preparation. Type out your talking points. You will be tempted not to do this, but if you type the talking points, you will script your dialogue and goals and help your team understand the business issues you must discuss. *Carry them with you and review them as you chat with the senior executive.* It will help you stay focused on your topics and meeting goals.

When holding your first twenty-minute meeting with a prospect on the phone or in-person always prepare specific talking points to manage your conversation (and any sales team member who is with you). Your talking points should include:

- Issues you want to communicate during the meeting

- Points you want your sales team members to avoid discussing

- The goal for the sales meeting

- The questions or sales objections you anticipate the prospect will ask or discuss

The questions or topics each team member will be responsible for answering

Following is a completed Talking Points Form to use as an example. In the Appendix, you will find a blank form you can copy and adapt to your needs.

Example

First Meeting Talking Points

Date Prepared:	4/17/2012
Sales Rep:	Shelly Smith
Prospect's Name:	Smith Doctors Group
Contacts:	Ralph Muller, CEO and Ian Muller, CTO
Business Type:	Healthcare software for patient management
Public/Private:	Private
# of Employees:	47
Business URL:	www.smithdoctors.com
Industry Business Pains:	Patient management; need to reduce their advertising expenses and increase revenue through alternative means.
Industry Terminology:	Board Certified, Clinical Research, Revenue Replacement Model, Human Capital Costs
Sales value proposition to communicate:	*We are Profit Improvement Specialists for physicians and specialty practices.* We help medical facilities automate their patient management, and increase the effectiveness of their advertising and marketing. • We offer the ability to automate patient management. • We use e-Zine newsletters for channel distribution. • We work with senior executives only.
Our Associates Talking Points:	Dan Kelley • On-line development process and opt-in e-mail usage • Executive briefing meeting
Areas to Avoid:	Had bad experience with direct mail; does not want to use third-party subcontractors
Meeting Goals:	Set up new 1-hour meeting; Budget; Time frame; Competition; Who is making the decision
Goal Time Period:	One Week
Potential Purchase:	Patient management software, e-Zine newsletter; consulting, opt-in e-mail
Value of Deal:	$50,000 this year
Additional Comments	The prospect is anxious to buy based on need to expand. He is not price resistant, but seeks value.

As part of your sales tool box, you should complete this form and hand it to each of your team members prior to the twenty-minute meeting.

The following are actual case histories of this program being presented to C-level executives.

Case History SVP Example – Relieving the Pain (Auto Industry Dealer Software)

In one case, I communicated the following:

> *Mr. VP, as indicated when you and I spoke on the phone, we specialize in **Profit Improvement for the Auto Dealership Industry**. We do this by helping senior executives like you automate their communication to their client base. We accomplish this through a premeditated briefing program where we analyze your business needs and then provide programs and services to help your firm increase top line revenue. The auto industry is moving from a decentralized distribution channel to a centralized channel, making it more difficult for mega dealers like yourself to maintain connectivity to your paying customers on a localized basis.*

So, what have I done?

1. I have reconfirmed my SVP and brand message.

2. I have established that we are knowledgeable specialists about the auto industry.

3. I have connected the prospect's business pain to our SVP and how our IT offering can help improve the company's business success.

SVP Example – Relieving the Prospect's Business Pain (Gaming Industry) Using IT as a Business Tool to Drive Results

In another case, I communicated the following:

> *Mr. VP, as discussed on the phone, we are Specialists in Casino Player Retention. We accomplish this by working with the property's senior management team to analyze player retention and then developing methodologies and systems to increase management controls of that revenue stream. We know the gaming industry is going through a difficult time with customer retention due to the diversification of gaming throughout the United States and there is increased demand to generate more gaming dollars per player.*

By using this model, you will be able bridge your introduction, your validation, and the communication of your SVP to the questioning (mining) of opportunities.

Once you have stated the above bridge, you will probably hear a question like *"How do you accomplish this casino player retention?"*

My response was *"We do this through an organized process where we analyze the casino's (or hotel's or insurance company's) systems to determine their effectiveness on player retention and their effect on revenue. Mr. VP, how is your firm handling this industry issue?"*

So, what have I done?

Instead of selling technology (like most IT companies do), I have focused on the industry's pain and then transferred that pain to the C-level executive in terms of revenue and expenses and how I use technology and professional services as tools to drive results.

When I transferred the industry's pain to the executive, I never directly said he had the same industry problems, but you can assume he would not have asked to meet me if he was not concerned about the same issues and intrigued by my SVP.

If you can find the pain, you can be a doctor and fix it. When a person is injured in a car accident, they never ask, *How much will it cost to get well?* Instead, the first thing they say is, *Get me the best doctor and take away the pain!*

Remember—you are not an IT salesperson—you're a strategic advisor who uses technology and professional services as a tool to drive business results.

Discussing the industry's pains (that statistically the prospect mostly likely shared) allowed the executive to save face and opened up the door for him to respond about his firm's personal needs (pain). By continuing to turn the prospect's pain into **income** and **expense issues or consequence management exposure**, I maintained my legitimate right to be talking to the C-level decision maker.

Being Professionally Blunt with the Prospect

During the twenty-minute meeting, be the doctor and be professionally blunt.

Most IT salespeople believe their communications must be subservient to prospects to get deals closed.

You want another demo? No problem.

You want me to write a technical specification document from scratch for free? Of course!

You would like me to redo the proposal for the fourth time? Sure.

Wrong!

To sell more IT and services to management, you must act like a doctor who tells the truth, not someone with a warm and fuzzy bedside manner.

Prospects do not have to like you to buy—they just have to trust you and believe your IT offering can help them increase their business success. An advanced sales method of selling IT to executives is to use a professionally blunt approach. Professionally blunt is not the same as being generally blunt—because that is rude. Being professionally blunt means talking to the prospect as a peer ... not as a vendor. Professionally blunt communications systematically separate your IT presentation from your competitor's—because you are not acting like a vendor.

When was the last time you told a C-level executive he or she was wrong? If you are truly a peer, and you say it correctly and professionally—you can tell executives they are wrong, and they will still buy IT from you.

To implement a professionally blunt communications approach, focus on being direct, like a doctor. If you are 400 pounds overweight, your doctor is going to tell you to stop eating pizza every night, stop drinking beer, and go run two miles a day. It may hurt your feelings, but this kind of advice will help you stay alive.

Similarly, when you are trying to sell IT or professional services to corporate executives and they are misinformed, under-informed, or not intelligent enough to grasp what technology is needed—tell them. For example:

> *"Ms. Prospect, I appreciate that you have bought this type of IT (services) before, but your acquisition process is not necessarily going to give you the results you are seeking. Here is what I recommend."*

> *"Mr. Prospect, your decision to go with company X is not the right direction for you."*

> *"Ms. Prospect, your observations about the IT offering you are considering are not accurate."*

Why does this work?

It works because by taking this path, you separate yourself from other IT salespeople who sound the same, act the same, and ultimately have to charge the same (because they are in commodity mode). Many salespeople do not understand that true advisors—advise! Don't just agree or concur with inaccurate statements made by an uninformed prospect. Help your prospect be successful. Stop being a salesperson and start being a true strategic consultant who helps prospects drive business results. You will sell more.

Be respectful, but be direct.

Case History – Using Psychological ROI to Open the Door*

I was selling an $850,000.00 software application to a large global insurance company headquartered in New England against two IT companies that were both global players. My technology offering was 40 percent higher in price than both of these competitors. The vice president who had the budget and was the contract signer almost had a heart attack when he saw my proposal pricing and almost immediately dismissed our offering as too much money. But after repeated attempts to reach him by email and phone, I finally connected with him and said, "Whatever you buy you are going to own for the next 10 years. Meet with me for 20 minutes—to make sure you are making the right investment. I will not waste your time."

He relented and gave me 20 more minutes.

As I sat down, the executive launched the conversation and started talking about our price as compared to my competitors', saying there was no use in discussing at length his investment in our IT offering.

---

*Using psychological ROI as a closing technique will be discussed in detail in Chapter 8.

I looked him in the eye and said, "Forget price. All things being equal, whose offering meets your needs more?"

He said, "Yours, of course, but I do not have the budget."

So I replied, "If you install the other companies on your short list, you will NOT meet your objectives, your investment is going to fail, and then you are going to have to explain to your senior management why it didn't work (psychological ROI*). Then you are going to have to spend money a second time to fix it. Why not find the funding now and bypass all these issues?"

Well, he did, and I got the sale.

Remember, B2B technology selling techniques to C-level executives and presidents of small companies need to be focused on four areas to be successful. They are:

- **Revenue improvement**

- **Expense reduction**

- **Consequence management/risk management**

- **Agility improvement**

If you are selling web development, ask yourself how the new website will increase revenues and/or decrease expenses.

If you are selling an enterprise CRM application, evaluate how the prospect will use your CRM system to increase corporate revenues and/or decrease expenses.

If you are selling professional services to a 3,000-person company, determine a model you can show on how your services will increase revenues and/or decrease department expenses.

If you talk about other areas, you will never be successful selling technology in volume. When C-level executives and presidents make decisions on technology, it <u>always comes back to revenues, expenses, agility, and risk management</u>. Focus on these four areas and watch your commissions increase. Many technology account salespeople focus too much on other features and benefits, and this affects the closing ratio.

Focus on the prospects' operational pain. Then, turn your technology service or product into doctor's medicine that will fix this pain with an increase in sales, a reduction in expenses, and/or better consequence management.

Preparing for the Twenty-Minute Meeting When It Is a Group Meeting

When your 20-minute meeting is a group presentation, it is important to realize every person invited has a reason to be there. Do not minimize the title of any person attending a demo. You are mining confirmation of the group as a whole about your (newly created) SVP. There is a tendency (even by very experienced technology salespeople) to ignore lower titled attendees and to play to the senior title in the room (many times your C-level contact). Doing this is a strategic sales mistake. This *faux pas* causes technology salespeople to lose many deals.

Using the *Value Forward Sales* method, we actively seek out C-level management to launch the sales cycle. But when presenting to a group in your first 20-minute meeting, where lower-level managers and attendees have been instructed to be there by your C-level contact, everyone should be treated equally. People with a manager's or a director's title may not make the decision, but when the steering committee regroups to make a decision, those decision influencers could sink you, just because you hurt their egos by ignoring them. Always ask questions of lower-level managers. There is ego in the boardroom and in a demo. You need to control lower-level managers who are trying to impress their boss by asking you questions that are cumbersome; ask them their opinions to make them feel important.

Holding a C-level meeting is like being on Broadway. It's also crowd control. Often in an IT presentation, you have assembled many title levels, each participant with unique needs and objectives. When the presentation is over, you may not get the opportunity to interact with the group as a team again. So, you have to grab all the audience members' attention simultaneously, paint a picture in their brains of how you want them as a group to remember you, and demonstrate your SVP and distinguish yourself from all other competitors.

Never let attendees see you sweat. If something goes wrong during an application, service discussion, or product demo, just keep moving. In many cases, prospects will not even notice a misstep in a high-level presentation as you quickly speed type on your laptop or redirect your conversation.

Remember, though, 50 percent of technology sales decisions are based on the quality of the demo, and perfection is expected. Focus on making a strong executive presentation.

As the meeting unfolds, ask open-ended questions of the group as a whole and of individuals specifically. When you ask directed questions, specifically use people's first names (remember, you collected their business cards at the beginning).

Prior to the meeting, *write out specific questions to ask each attendee.* You need to focus on connecting with the like skill set person in the room (i.e., ask senior technical people technical questions). Even if you know the answers, it helps initiate an interactive conversation and it makes the attendees feel welcome.

Sales mining questions start with the following lead words:

- **How**
- **Why**
- **Do you**
- **When**
- **Will you**
- **How long**
- **Can we**
- **What**

The key to getting answers from decision makers is to keep asking questions. If you continually ask the questions **WHY** and **HOW**, you will be more successful.

Executive	We don't outsource software development
Salesperson	How come your firm doesn't outsource IT development?
Executive	Our company considered implementing new retail software, but we decided as an executive team against it.
Salesperson	Why is your firm not interested in increasing profits?
Executive:	We need to automate our HR system.
Salesperson:	Why? How quickly will you make that decision?
Executive:	We are thinking about staying with our current vendor.
Salesperson:	Why? How has that current vendor performed for you?
Executive:	Our CEO wants us to focus on a redesign of our website.
Salesperson:	Why? How will you make a vendor selection?

Executive:	We are considering installing a new CRM system.
Salesperson:	Why? How can we help you install that CRM system?

Small Company Sales

In small company sales, the Sales Miner Approach is even more effective—and dangerous. Many of the attendees in the meeting may be related, so always respect everyone in the room. Ask the questions *"why"* and *"how"* cautiously.

Your 20 Minutes Are Up

As you hit the self-imposed 20-minute time barrier, keep talking if the executive is asking you questions about your technology services and business results. It is the executive's time, and you are there to develop a peer-to-peer relationship.

But remember, transactional selling is the key to increased IT sales and greater commissions—not hanging on to prospects who are not prepared to take an action step to buy.

After 30 minutes, you should wrap up and recap in quick detail the pains the executive has identified for you that exist in his or her firm and how your IT offering can help improve the company's success.

If the prospect has answered your transactional sales qualifying questions correctly:

Look the executive in the eye and say:

> *Mr./Ms. CFO, I appreciate the time you have*
> *spent with me. Based on my commitment to*
> *take no more than 20 minutes of your time,*
> *what I would like to do is set up a new*
> *appointment for our management teams to*
> *discuss in more detail how we can increase*
> *your business revenue (or decrease expenses*
> *or manage risks) using our programs. We*
> *usually do this in an executive briefing format*
> *with you and other executive team members. It*
> *will take only one hour.*
>
> *When would be a good day?*

If you have positioned your SVP correctly, the executive will set up an appointment. If the executive hesitates, wait for a response.

If the executive says he or she is not really interested in meeting again at this time, ask why. If he or she has been discussing pain management with you, there should not be any logical reason for this prospect not to see you again.

Once you hear your prospect's objection, focus on the pain and then communicate again your firm's process to eliminate it. Act surprised that he or she would not want to explore with you at another appointment more detailed methods to increase revenues or reduce expenses.

Again, ask for the second appointment, telling the executive you will not waste his or her time.

Studies consistently show that salespeople who continually ask for an appointment from a qualified prospect get them. Ask the executive at least **THREE** times for the next appointment—every time slightly changing your request method.

Remember, if you have done your homework, you are sitting in front of a decision maker who has a pain that needs to be fixed.

If after 20 minutes you have determined that this prospect is not a qualified buyer because they cannot answer your transactional questions correctly, or they say they are not interested in your business success tools, respond by saying:

> *Mr./Ms. Prospect, thank you for your time today. It seems like we are not a good fit right now. Can I follow-up with you in the future to see if things change?*

Then leave, place them into a passive marketing model and follow-up with them once a month until the buying cycle and the selling cycle meet.

Don't waste time with unqualified buyers.

 TIP The first appointment with the C-level executive or the president of a small company should always be a conceptual business discussion.

PowerPoint Presentations

Generally, PowerPoint presentations are not used during the first 20-minute appointment, for several reasons.

- It is distracting to the decision maker.

- It is difficult to maintain your self-imposed 20-minute time allocation, and you will waste valuable time setting up and taking down your PC.

- It makes the appointment with the C-level executive seem more like a sales call than a discussion among equals.

Remember, the 20-minute appointment is a conceptual sale to get the executive briefing.

Highlights of this section:

- In technology sales, experienced sales executives *do not wing it.*

- The goal of your 20-minute meeting is to qualify the prospect.

- You must work with prospects who have the potential to buy within your normal selling timeline.

- To sell larger deals more effectively, use an engagement outline.

- Never let a prospect see you sweat. If something goes wrong during an application, service discussion, or product demo, just keep moving. In many cases, prospects will not even notice a misstep.

Exercises:

1. To manage sales objections, develop a top 10 sales objection talking points document. Print it, keep it with you at all times and review it before every meeting.

2. Prepare mining questions to review before your next appointment.

3. Prepare a Client Engagement Outline to use with your next deal.

Chapter

5

Giving an Executive Briefing and Whiteboard Presentation That Makes Prospects Buy

After reading this chapter, you will learn:

- How to present to prospects using an interactive whiteboard format

- How to make your webinar more successful

Since releasing the first publication of this book in 2001, I have received many emails and letters from IT sales executives and high tech CEOs from around the world about my Three Box Monty™ whiteboard presentation method—testimonials on how using the structured format of the three boxes has helped them close $100,000.00, $500,000.00, $1 million and $10 million technology, software, and professional services deals.

Follow this method—study its techniques and practice what you are going to say—and you can double your sales closing ratio using this one sales technique.

Fifty percent of all technology sales are made in the executive briefing presentation step of a sales cycle. So, if you cannot give a strong executive presentation, your sales success will be minimal. Executive briefings are like being on stage—you must know your part and the other actors' parts as well, and you must be prepared for any unexpected event that may happen. You're going to get only one chance.

Executive Briefing Talking Points Script

So, the day has come. We have cold called the C-level executive with our SVP and have convinced him or her that we are specialists. We have held our 20-minute mining conversation (meeting), have qualified the prospect, and have been given a one-hour executive briefing appointment time to talk to the executive team in detail.

You are up to bat. What do you do? Again, the key to the *Value Forward Sales* method is that you are always prepared. Selling IT is a premeditated sport. If you are using team selling, the first thing to do is to get everyone together who is involved in the meeting's presentation and chat about the format, the prospect, and the presentation's pain concept.

Best Methods to Present to Fortune 1000 Executives and Small Business Presidents

The goal of your executive briefing is to get more information on what your prospect's needs are, to match up your IT offering's capabilities to meet the prospect's needs, to prequalify the buyer, and to set up a sales cycle selling timeline that forces the prospect to buy transactionally within your sales quota success timeline, proving to you this prospect is not wasting your valuable selling time.

Depending on the technology, software, or professional services you sell, after the executive briefing is completed, you will take one of three steps: 1) set up your next meeting and hold a more detailed prospect demo, specifications, or scope meeting; 2) create a proposal and submit it personally to the executive team; or 3) put the prospect into a passive engagement marketing model to follow up on a monthly basis until the prospect becomes a qualified buyer.

I can't count the number of times I have sat with a client's experienced sales team members observing their executive briefing demonstration skills, only to see them fumble and wing it through their presentations. They fail to qualify the management team, and they start a sales cycle that will be buried in a sales forecast, with no end in sight and no signed agreement.

Right now, determine that you will never wing it and that you will be a pro. Follow these proven guidelines for your executive briefing, and you will be successful.

Pre-Briefing Team Meeting Guidelines

1.   You are the technology salesperson. Your commission is riding on this executive briefing. You are responsible for how this meeting goes and for what your staff should or should not say to your prospect and the management team in the executive briefing room. **THIS IS YOUR SHOW.** You need to tell everyone who is on your presenting team how the process is going to evolve. **DO NOT** let an operations person, a support manager, or your boss dictate how this meeting's agenda will develop or how the presentation will go. Never let a senior executive from your company manage your executive briefing—when you lose the deal, this person will have executive amnesia, forgetting what he or she said and blaming you for the lost deal. <u>It is your commission</u>. Control the room and the briefing—don't let your team wing it.

2.   Create an internal agenda for your team prior to your meeting on who will speak on what subjects. List their names beside the subject matter with a time sequence on your **Talking Points Script**.

3.   Assign a maximum time for each part the speaker is allocated to use.

4.   Accept that as the salesperson, you should **<u>NOT</u>** do most of the talking.

5.   Review with your team what PowerPoint presentation you will use, if any. Print hard copies of the PowerPoint presentation along with the

agenda and insert them into folders. Hand a folder to each of your team members and include the contact names, telephone numbers, time of the meeting, and the street directions.

6.   Make sure you list a participant's name next to each PowerPoint slide so that all presenters on your team know what they are responsible for and each individual is able to explain his or her assigned slides' details.

7.   In your Talking Points Script, list who will answer the prospect's question on each specific subject. Generally, if there is a technical question, the salesperson should be quiet (even if he or she knows the answer). Let your technical people respond. Remember, peer to peer.

8.   In your executive pre-meeting with your team, create the **Top 10 Tough Questions** your prospect may ask you (and your team) during your presentation, including the questions you fear most. Then as a team, determine an answer for each question and who will respond.

9.   If you are presenting screen shots of software, always bring a backup PC preloaded with your application, just in case.

10.   Try never to present live software in an executive briefing. Instead, show screen shots of great reports and client deliverables.

11.   In your executive briefing, generally the salesperson handles the presenters' **introductions,**

the **company overview**, the **SVP**, the **industry's pains, the pains expressed by the C-level executive, requests for pricing**, and the **wrap-up.**

12. In your meeting, the operations/professional service team members are responsible for **technical descriptions of applications, application skill sets review,** training discussions, and **delivery time schedules.**

If you have operations or professional service team members attend your prospect executive meetings, teach them **never to say no** in the meeting. Teach them to say, *"That's a possibility. Can we get back to you on it?"* By their very nature, operational staffs are conservative and never want to try anything new. All technology sales custom requests have a price. Let management make that decision, not some operations person who is worried he or she is already too busy.

Be a sales and market driven technology company, not a technology driven company.

Executive Presentation Talking Points

Lead Presenter's Name (salesperson):_____
Client's name_____
Client's URL_____
Client's Address/Briefing Location_____

Briefing Date_____Briefing Time_____
Time Allocated to Briefing by Client_____

Meeting Lead Attendee:
Name_____ Title_____Telephone_____

Meeting Attendees:
Name_____ Title_____Telephone_____
Name_____ Title_____Telephone_____
Name_____ Title_____Telephone_____

Client's Pain Issues_____

Product or Service To Be Presented_____

Presenter's Name_____
Title_____
Responsible for Presentation Slide (List slide number/subject)_____

Presenter's Name_____
Title_____
Responsible for Presentation Slide (List slide number/subject)_____

Presenter's Name_____
Title_____
Responsible for Presentation Slide (List slide number/subject)_____

Presenter's Name_____
Title_____
Responsible for Slide/Whiteboard Presentation (List slide number/subject)_____

Goal of Presentation_____
_____

What does the prospect want to see/hear at the meeting?_____

Current product/service being used by the prospect_____
_____

Current business pain with existing product or service_____
_____

What do we want to sell them?_____

What is the dollar value for the first year?_____

What is the dollar value of this client over the next three years?_____

Do they have a budget?   _____Yes   _____No

If yes, how much?_____

When do they want this product or service?_____

Why will they buy from us?_____

Why will we lose this deal?_____

Which contact is signing the purchase order/contract?_____

Which contact(s) is (are) making the decision?_____

Is there a consultant involved?   _____Yes   _____No
          If yes, what is the consultant's name?_____
          Consultant's company name_____
          Consultant's telephone_____
          Is the consultant: For us_____ Against us_____ Neutral_____

What are the prospect's business consequences if they do
not buy from us?_____
_____

What does the selling team need to do to close this business?_____
_____

Are there any unusual marketing expenses needed to close this business?_____
_____

Next Action Steps_____

Small Business Sales

The aforementioned format is also a good guideline for small
business technology sales if you are doing a solo
demonstration. It will help you maintain a logical progression

in thought when you present. Studies of sales presentation methods show that when two or more people make a presentation, statistically they have a higher closing ratio than one presenter. So, even if you are a small technology sales organization, you may want try a team sale to increase your sales success.

The Three Box Monty—A Better Way to Present to Senior Level Executives

Most senior level executives have seen enough PowerPoint presentations to last two lifetimes. Due to the over-proliferation of this communication method, presenting methods are reverting **BACK** to the whiteboard.

New studies from professional seminar associations are indicating the whiteboard process gets a higher retention and a more positive approval rating than PowerPoint.

To energize your prospect presentations (even if you are demonstrating software), cut back on the computer presentation and start interacting in a demonstrative way using the whiteboard (providing there is one in the room in which you are meeting).

 TIP The whiteboard presentation works extremely well when you are competing against large, established technology players. Usually their presentations are PowerPoint driven and TOO SLICK. Often their demonstration materials are corporately produced, very rigid in design, and built on a 30- to 40-card deck presentation.

One-Hour Executive Briefing Using the Three Box Monty Whiteboard Format

---

Three Box Monty
Executive Presentation Format
Length: 1 - 1½ hours

Team Prep	Minutes
• Presenter group arrives at least 30 minutes early. Meets in parking lot.	30

Presentation

		Minutes
1.	Presenter introductions/business cards are handed out.	**2.5**
2.	Introduce attendees.	**2.5**
3.	Lead presenter (salesperson) confirms the amount of time available for the presentation.	--
4.	Lead presenter reconfirms the business pains expressed by the management contact coupled with industry pains.	**5**
5.	Lead presenter launches into slide presentation (eight slides or fewer) giving company history, client list, and SVP.	**10**
6.	Three Box Monty presentation (depending on if you have an IT product or a specialized service to explain).	**15-30**
7.	Optional step: Service or product presenter launches into a screen shot or reports presentation of what is being sold. If not, move on to Step 8.	**15-30**
8.	Executive Briefing Close	**10**
	Client Q&A. Wrap-up. Ask transactional questions of the senior executive to confirm he/she is still qualified.	

Using this format, you will eliminate presentation issues that often come up, including, but not limited to:

- Presenters showing up late

- C-level attendees deciding to stay only 30 minutes and not informing you

- Not remembering the names of the attendees who were at the meeting, and not knowing what their titles are

- Having multiple presenters respond to tough questions differently

- Not leaving enough time for the demo and Q&A

- Your presenting team not looking or acting like a team

Again, do not wing this part of the presentation. Think it through, plan and develop a process, and practice it. The best method I have used for this kind of presentation is as follows:

1. Go to the whiteboard and draw three rectangles. Have two boxes situated next to each other on a straight line and the third box centered below the other two (see example).

2. Inside the first box, print the name of the prospect's industry (Health Care, Retail, Manufacturing, Insurance, etc.).

3. Inside the second box, print your prospect company's name (Toys Inc., Trucks Inc., etc.).

4. Inside the third box centered below the top two boxes, print your company's name (Value Forward, etc.).

5. Under the first box (industry), start listing in bullet format the public issues of business pain the industry

is experiencing based on your previous third party research. Be broad, but list items that are generally well known and have been documented in industry publications or on specific industry association websites.

6. Under the second box (prospect's company), list in bullet format the business pains that were discussed during your first 20-minute meeting. Standing at the whiteboard, state publicly who during your first meeting said these are company business pains (e.g., Dan Smith said during my first meeting that your firm is experiencing …). Verbally identifying where this information came from gives you power in the room and negates anyone disagreeing with you or feeling defensive because you are talking about his or her department.

7. Now ask the room if there are any other "events" going on in the business in this area that have not been identified.

8. Once the prospect has completed making comments, under the third box (your company), list the business pain and issues your professional services, software, or technology offerings will fix for the prospect.

9. **With the executive team in the room, discuss how your IT offerings will fix their company business pains, linking your offerings to their needs and their industry's barriers to success.**

10. Remember, we are working with senior level executives. Make sure the issues that are listed under all the boxes can somehow be turned into **income** and

expenses pain management or consequence management controls.

This is an interactive presentation that looks spontaneous but is obviously premeditated. So, don't do all the talking; be quiet at times and let your prospects speak.

As soon as anyone in the room starts giving answers, start writing his or her responses under the box with the prospect company's name on it. If the person is longwinded, **hand him or her the whiteboard marker**, and ask him or her to explain.

Now step back and listen.

Handing the whiteboard marker to one of the prospects in the audience works especially well if one of the prospect's management team members has a difficult or challenging personality. Let this person sell your concept for you by writing on the board and allowing his or her ego to be a participant in your presentation.

8. When you have completed the discussion about each box, just connect all the boxes with an arrow.

Example

Smith Software
Profit Improvement Specialist for
Physicians and Speciality Practices

1

Healthcare Industry

- 36% of healthcare facilities spend too much on electricity

- 3 out of 4 healthcare organizations need to increase their A/R collections from delinquent paying patients

- 79% of healthcare companies need better patient management software

- Most hospital CFOs invest only in capital equipment that controls labor costs

- Only 17% of healthcare facilities are HIPPA compliant

2

ABC Physician Facility

- Increase income by reducing A/R collections

- Reduce labor costs related to filing insurance paperwork

- Increase revenue through onsite pharmaceutical sales

- Increase revenue through better appointment management

3

Smith Software

- Install new software application to automate insurance claims

- Install automated telephone collection system for patient collection

- Train physicians on revenue management

The Goal of Your Three Box Monty White Board Presentation

The goal of the Three Box Monty is to *re-qualify* your prospects into taking **transactional sales steps** that move them forward in your sales cycle. During your presentation, make sure you ask these questions again to the senior executives, as always, using a conversational tone:

1. Do you have a budget for this project?
2. When will the decision be made?
3. Who will be making the decision with you?
4. What other companies are you speaking with?
5. If you decide to move forward, who will be signing our paperwork?
6. When do you want to be operational?
7. How do you see our IT offering helping your firm?

Depending on the technology, software, or professional services you sell (managed services, staff augmentation, electronic components, enterprise application, SaaS, etc.), at this point if the prospects are still qualified, you will proceed to your next action step. Depending on what you sell, you will set up either a new, elongated appointment to give a detailed software demo or another meeting to develop a client scope/specifications outline. If the prospect is ready to buy, you will immediately develop a proposal (to be submitted by hand—not email).

Reintroduce your client engagement outline at this juncture, and use it again as a prospect talking tool. Remember to use our transactional selling model—take new selling action steps only if the prospect is qualified. Sell buyers ... not lookers.

By using our Value Forward Sales whiteboard method, Three Box Monty, you have accomplished four things:

1. Made your presentation interactive based on the prospect's needs

2. Positioned yourself as a specialist—not a generalist

3. Subliminally educated the prospects on your ability to fix **THEIR** pain using your technology to drive results

4. Re-qualified them as prospects in a buying cycle

Use this sales process and you will close more deals. Don't get too sophisticated with your whiteboard drawing because that would have the same effect as the too-slick PowerPoint. Your objective is to make the entire process less vendor-driven and more buyer-driven.

Tips for successful whiteboard presentations:

1. Standing at the board while your prospects are sitting down and listening gives you a superior-subordinate position over them physically and psychologically. By standing above them, you are the teacher and they are the students. That's why the aggressive prospect in the demo room will quiet down when you hand him or her the whiteboard marker to put his or her thoughts on the board. Now instead of feeling subordinated and insecure, this person gets to stand up and feel equal to you again.

2. When speaking from a standing position, always repeat <u>important</u> messages **twice**. When saying the message the second time, lean forward with emphasis and speak half as fast as you did the first time.

We are specialists in Milestone Management!

We are specialists in Milestone Management!

3. Take public speaking courses to reinforce your IT sales training skills. Remember, if you are selling to a room full of executives, they are all taking notes and then going back to their offices. You need to leave a UNIQUE SVP in their minds (and in their notes) they will recall. So, when they regroup as a decision team or a steering committee, they will remember you and your firm favorably.

Case History – Small Business Presentation Variation

I was meeting with the president and the CFO of a 50-person company in their conference room to sell them software development. As soon as I finished my company overview and our SVP, I went to the whiteboard and drew the three boxes.

Then I handed the president the marker and asked him what problems (technology pains) he saw facing the small business owner in his industry. He went to the board and started listing the industry's issues under the industry box.

We chatted about what the president wrote, and when he was done, I handed the marker to the CFO and asked him what issues and problems he was experiencing. The CFO started listing those pains under his company's box (remember, income and expense control).

With that completed, I went to my firm's box and listed how we could fix these pains. Then I connected the three boxes with arrows. By having the C-level executives in this small firm visualize with me their problems and my firm's ability to be a doctor to fix their problems, I simultaneously eliminated all my competition and won the deal.

Case History – Fortune 1000 Presentation

A team of three support and operations staff members and I were presenting at one of the largest retail discount department store chains in the world at its corporate headquarters.

There were 20 people in the room, including the CFO, the CIO, and the CTO. The CTO was well recognized in the business magazines as a world leader in technology visioning, and he was the dominant personality in the room.

So, I went through the steps of the Three Box Monty listed above. During our meeting, the CTO was aggressive in his questioning about my SVP and what made us different. At the opening of the presentation, I did a five-slide PowerPoint presentation about our background, our customers, and my central SVP. As each slide was presented, the CTO asked detailed, long-winded questions, probing and pushing for details.

At the end of the five-slide presentation, I went to the board and drew the three boxes, listing the industry's pains, and then I turned to the CTO and said, *"Mr. CTO, what additional pain is your industry experiencing?"*

Mr. CTO got up and started a 10-minute dissertation of the industry's technology issues. As he spoke, he listed on the board these issues under the industry box. When he was finished (and still standing at the whiteboard), I said, *"Mr. CTO, what industry issues is your firm experiencing?"*

Mr. CTO then proceeded to list his firm's issues under his company's box. Simultaneously, the CTO started asking for input from his management team sitting in the audience. So, as I stood there next to the CTO in the front of the room of this multibillion-dollar company, he started drawing on my whiteboard, talking about how his retail conglomerate and my software company would interface our applications, convincing himself and his team on how our two companies could work together. When the CTO was done, I listed and discussed our pain management features under our box and then connected them with arrows.

As soon as I had connected the three boxes, the CTO got up from his seat again, went to the whiteboard, and laid out the complete integration of my technology and their technology for his management team. Guess who got the deal? I did.

The whiteboard method works. Try it. You will win more technology deals!

How to Give Three Box Monty Webinar Presentations

Ten Steps to Make Your Webinar More Successful

1. Accept that webinars are invisible selling. You must engage your prospects with multiple sensory devices in your webinar to get them to focus on your IT offering. The more sensory devices you use, the more they will see your IT offering's intrinsic value subliminally. Use pop-up video testimonials or audio testimonials to add depth to the presentation.

2. Keep all first Three Box Monty webinars under one hour.

3. Use the same format as the whiteboard Three Box Monty in your webinar. Do not have the three boxes pre-drawn, but instead hand-draw the boxes on the screen as you interact with the prospect.

4. Submit an agenda in writing to participants ahead of time.

5. When launching your webinar, ask when your prospect signs in who else is listening and what their titles are. This helps you know and manage who is monitoring your presentation.

6. When people check in to your presentation, confirm that each person can see the screen and tell everyone what they should see in the right hand corner. Some prospects, even technically astute prospects, don't like to admit when the technology on their PC is not working.

7. Ask at least one question of your attendees for every two slides you show.

8. Slow down. You should spend approximately two minutes per slide. Slides are talking points—not reading points.

9. Always ask the seven qualifying questions, as listed previously in my description of the Three Box Monty. Remember to use a conversational tone.

10. Remember, the goal of your webinar is to qualify prospects and to determine the next action step they will take with you in tandem (detailed software demo, scope development, proposal, etc.) to prove to you they are transactional sales prospects in a buying mode.

Technology Demos in Executive Briefings

Having sold tens of millions of dollars of software, technology, and professional services to small businesses and Fortune 1000 companies, I have come to develop several direct methods on how a software demo should be presented. I recommend in the executive meeting to try <u>not</u> to do live software demos. But if you do, follow these guidelines:

1. If you are looking at your laptop screen, you are not talking to your prospects. You are the salesperson. You need to focus on interactively speaking with the prospect, not hitting keyboard strokes. If you are selling a software application, never do the demo yourself. Bring a sales engineer or an operations person who can do the demo (based on your scripted

talking points instructions) and focus on showing
screen shots only of flashy reports.

2. If there are senior executives in the room, do not
spend more than 30 minutes on the software demo
unless they ask to see the details. Demo and explain
the value you have, **but do not present live software**.
Instead, always show flashy screen shots. They will
get bored if you spend longer than 30 minutes. Show
the flash, talk the rest.

3. If the presentation demo flickers, locks up, or does not
operate as expected, don't sweat it. Don't let your
demo engineer announce to the room that something
is wrong. Just keep moving. If you worry about it, the
prospects will worry about it. If it is obvious to the
prospect, just say, *"Sorry, it's a demo system,"* and
keep moving.

4. As the salesperson, pay attention while your sales
engineer is doing the demo. I know you have seen this
software demo a million times, but watch your
prospect. Read your prospect. Also, don't type notes
about your prospect's comments into a laptop. It is
very disrespectful and distracting, and again, you are
looking away from the prospect.

5. Never hand out marketing brochures until the end.
Not having a brochure to read focuses customers to
listen to you, to take notes, and to pay attention to the
software presentation.

6. Remember, every person in the room is important
when it comes to closing this technology sale. While
the demo is going on, be sure to prod each one of

them with several questions (talking points) on his or her area of interest or responsibilities.

7. During executive briefings, make sure you leave enough of the allocated time for questions and answers. Sometimes we are so impressed with what our software can do that we just keep demonstrating until there is no time left to chat with the prospects.

I have been up against tough competition all my life. I wouldn't know how to get along without it. –Walt Disney

Value Forward Sales – Touch Management Program

So, you have completed your 20-minute appointment and 3 Box Monty, and you have scheduled specific new appointments based on your mined opportunities with the C-level executive.

Now is the time to develop your peer-to-peer interaction with the executive and his or her team, using strong communication skills. Due to the increase of communication technology (cell phones, email, pagers, etc.), some of the elementals of person-to-person communication are being lost. It is surprising how many basic sales skills some professional salespeople are lacking. If you have made it this far with the C-level executive, you need to keep this person near and dear to you and use him or her as the decision maker and possibly as a business coach. Maintaining this relationship will require frequent communication.

Under the <u>Touch Management Program</u>, we contact every person we meet during the sales cycle program **once a week until the buying cycle and the selling cycle intersect**.

To accomplish this, I recommend you have your marketing team develop a series of customer contact devices to be sent to each contact with whom you are negotiating. The Touch Management Program is different from other marketing communication in that it is specifically designed to be delivered **DURING THE SALES CYCLE** on a weekly basis. Communication devices may include a press release, a pre-developed sales letter, a webinar, or a business case study, etc.

The key is to touch every person within the prospect company every week during the sales cycle with your name and your firm's name, along with your marketing message.

This is a "light" Touch Management Program in that you are not personally calling every day. Instead, your marketing is making the contact for you. This program does not absolve you of the responsibility to keep following up in person (at least once a week), but it will help you bridge from personal meeting to meeting.

Persistence in selling and marketing = more sales.

Touch Management – Aggressive

So, you have completed your presentation, and one of two things has happened:

1. The prospect loved your SVP and wants a proposal (or depending on what kind of IT offering you sell, a more detailed software demo,

scope, or specifications meeting with techies in the room); or

2.   The prospect will get back to you.

Either way, before you leave, ask the senior managers in the room, *"What is the next step?"*

Don't be shy—you are talking to senior managers. Be direct—they are. They talk about business all day, so get to the point. You have value, too.

If they say they would like to get a proposal, **do not** ask to whom to send it.

Always hand-deliver your proposal if you can. Email reduces your closing ratio. If you have pre-qualified the prospect correctly, you should be justified budget-wise in giving the proposal to the prospect in person. If the deal size is too small and does not warrant an on-site presentation, or if the prospect says, *"No just send it to me,"* say the following:

> *Mr./Ms. Prospect, my management does not allow me to hand out proposals. What we do with clients like yourself is set up a "proposal webinar" to explain our offering in detail and to answer any questions you may have.*

Then set up your proposal as a 10-slide webinar and go through your offering's value and price. When you are done and have talked with the prospect in detail about what you sell and its investment—then email the written document.

If the prospect says, *"Thank you for your time; we will get back to you,"* while you are still seated around the conference table (less intimidating), ask the C-level in the room, *"Do you think there is a good fit for our two firms to work together?"* Listen carefully. He or she may be seeking input from others and just wants to regroup at a private meeting to get their input. Or the executive may not be interested and is waiting to tell you in an easier format (like on the phone).

Remember, **50 percent** of all technology sales are made or lost during the executive presentation. It's like crowd control—after your meeting, they all go back to their offices and become a decentralized thinking team again.

Control the executive briefing and the room—and you control the sale.

So, if you are selling software, professional services, web development, or project work, this is it. This is not a time to be passive. If you leave the boardroom without a strong perception of how it went, you lose.

If you still get a weak response, you probably did not present well.

Ask the C-level executive three more questions:

1.   *"Mr./Ms. C, is there any additional information my firm could supply you to help you consider our company?"*

2.   *"How can we work together?"* (Pull out your client engagement outline and discuss the premeditated steps you recommend you both take in tandem to be successful.)

3. *"Mr./Ms. C, would you like to get a proposal from us?"*

Ask these questions to prod for more feedback on where you stand. Nobody wants to spend time and effort on a proposal for a prospect who is not interested. The executive's response is what we are seeking. We need to understand his or her hesitation to address the objections and make the sale.

When you sell to C-level executives, it is important to have confidence. It's a hard skill set to teach. We often meet senior IT salespeople in our client engagements that lack confidence in themselves and in their communication capabilities to sell in the boardroom. Remember, no one knows more about your IT offering's value than you do—be proud of what you sell, and ask business to business questions of executives. It's your sales commission at stake.

Just because someone has a business title or works for a large worldwide conglomerate does not mean that person knows what he or she is doing. Think about all the dumb business mistakes IT senior management teams have made—and where are they today. Companies like Prime, Basic Four, Digital, Columbia Computers, and Cado are all just technology company memories of the past.

You are now in an executive world with the decision makers and the decision influencers. Ask the TOUGH QUESTIONS politely and professionally—but be direct.

Ask for their business now!

Touch Management Follow-Up

After the meeting, send **everyone** a thank you note, reconfirming the following:

1. Your SVP

2. The industry's pains

3. Your prospect's pains as illustrated on the whiteboard

4. Your firm's ability to fix those pains

5. The next steps outlined in the meeting

Make the letter no longer than two pages and send it in a <u>Priority Mail envelope</u> (two-day delivery). It will get noticed because of the heavy cardstock envelope, and it is less expensive than overnight delivery. Don't send an email.

Remember that when you do an executive briefing, send a letter, or have a meeting with your targeted prospect, you are subliminally communicating how your IT, software, or professional services are deployed. If your interaction with prospects pre-sale is sloppy, unprofessional, or not organized, you are implying to them that after the sale, your IT installation and support will be sloppy, unprofessional, or not organized.

When using the Touch Management Program between the first appointment and the second, if you are sending letters to managers you were directed to work with by your C-level contact, always send a copy ("cc") to the C-level executive to keep him or her informed about your ongoing communication with his or her company. Using the "cc" method will help you keep the dialogue between you and the executive open and direct.

Highlights of this section:

- The goal of the Three Box Monty is to *re-qualify* your prospects.

- Talk about business results, not features and functions.

- Fifty percent of all technology sales are made in the executive briefing presentation step of a sales cycle.

- Cut back on computer presentations and increase your interaction with the prospect.

- Continue contacting every person you meet during the sales cycle program at least once a week (Touch Management Program).

Exercises:

1. Experiment with a whiteboard and learn to feel comfortable drawing on it and working with it.

2. Role-play a Three Box Monty presentation with one of your colleagues. Also, role-play a webinar presentation with one of your colleagues.

3. When you find yourself planning a meeting with several team members, prepare a talking points script so everyone can participate on the topics about which they are most knowledgeable.

4. Send thank you notes to the executives of all meetings you have had recently. If there are deals that have stalled, send thank you notes to those executives reconfirming your SVP, industry pains and your ability to fix those pains.

Chapter

6

Is the Value Forward IT Sales Method Not Complex Enough?

After reading this chapter, you will learn:

- Four common mistakes salespeople make in complex sales

- How to manage lower level prospects

So far, you have penetrated the no talk zone of C-level executives as an industry specialist, met and communicated your value based on buyer drivers, qualified executives transactionally, managed your selling time better, and done a white board executive briefing that was interactive and focused on helping technology buyers see you as a trusted and strategic advisor.

I know, you sell big, expensive IT deals to multi-national companies and you think that there needs to be more in a selling method to succeed, right?

Wrong.

The concept of a complex IT sale is that you – the salesperson – make it complex.

- You deal with lower level decision influencers, not decision makers too often.

- You don't ask qualified questions early enough in your sales cycle

- You don't force prospects to take transactional sales steps with you to prove to you they are qualified

- You hope lower level managers who meet with you on a regular basis will communicate your value and manage your FAQs as brilliantly as you would and introduce you to their boss.

- You don't cold call—so you take any lead you can get (tradeshow, marketing, etc.) and fill up your sales pipeline with unqualified opportunities

- You confuse meeting activity and visibility in an account as forward movement in your sales cycle

- You think hope is an IT sales success strategy

The fact is, IT sales are only complex when you the IT salesperson do not manage the multiple layers of a large account opportunity the same way you manage a business opportunity of a lesser value.

To be honest, most salespeople spend more time selling their management team on how complex their big sale is…then the time they actually spend selling the big sale.

How to Sell Six, Seven and Eight Figure IT Deals Using the Value Forward IT Sales Method

Selling a $10 million enterprise software application, a $1.5 million project management deal, or a $850,000 telecommunications package to a Global 1000 company with a steering committee or a review team spread out over three countries is no different than selling a $80,000 deal to the CFO of a privately held machinery company that does less than $50 million in annual revenues.

I know, it is hard to believe—but true.

In fact, the 3T sales model of using Trust, Transactional and Time Management methods are even more important in larger transaction sales to be successful.

The more layers of lookers and buyers you have in a sales cycle, the more complex it becomes for you as the salesperson if you do not manage the selling process.

If your sales process is managed by the buyer, then they control your action steps to be implemented, your ability to communicate your value and ultimately your time management.

So why do you let buyers manage your commissions?

Is it because your pipeline is so narrow that you accelerate the importance of every opportunity and you just become subservient to every prospect's whim and instruction…because you need the sale?

When there are multiple decision makers and influencers in a large key account sale, you need to start at the top. You need to qualify them continuously. You need to make them take action steps with you in tandem so they prove to you that they are not wasting your time and you need to focus on the executive drivers that make them buy…or else you will have a complex sale where the buyer is controlling your commissions.

The biggest deal I ever sold was a $25+ million software application sale to a large conglomerate using the 3T sales process and the Value Forward method.

- Were there multiple levels of looks and buyers? Yes.

- Was there multiple geographies and time zone demos and discussions that I had to manage? Yes.

- Were there prospect contacts who tried to control my commissions by changing my sales steps? Of course.

- Were there lower level managers more interested in my features, functions and price than more "value"? Yes.

- Did they ask me to discount aggressively to get that deal? You bet.

- When I showed them my engagement outline at first, did they say, "we don't do it that way"? Yes.

Often, sales teams and the executive management staff struggle with their approach to what they call complex selling. The term "complex" is defined by Merriam-Webster Dictionary as: "composed of two or more parts and is hard to separate, analyze, or solve."

So what is a complex selling environment? A complex sale happens when there are multiple participants, sometimes located in different geographies all directly or indirectly actively involved in the decision process to buy a product or service.

Four Mistakes Most Salespeople Make in Complex Sales to Large Key Accounts

Today, most IT salespeople incorrectly define complex sales and this affects their ability to close business an increase corporate revenue.

1. Salespeople assume that if they are interacting with lower level managers who like or approve of their offering, then the prospect is qualified and in an active buyer mode.

This mistake complicates a sale because lower level contacts are professional lookers who will meet with vendors just to look busy. To be qualified, prospects must have management buy-in with funding approved and the prospect must take action steps during the sales cycle to prove they are qualified buyers.

2. The best way to sell companies is through lower level managers because they are more accessible than senior management.

This is a mistake because your first entry point into a company dictates how the prospect sees you. If your first contact is a lower level manager below the title of Vice President (in the US), you are perceived to be a commodity before your sales cycle starts.

3. Salespeople give equal weight to working with lower level managers as they do with senior management and hope lower level contacts will induce senior management to buy.

This is a mistake because lower level associates may suggest, recommend, or approve...but they normally don't buy quickly. Giving equal time and sales cycle support to lower level prospects implies that you do not know how to get to senior management. The result is that you lose control of your sales cycle. Often without a proven sales process, sales teams in complex sales just take the least path of resistance to show their management team they are doing something by talking to anybody who will listen.

4. Salespeople believe that lower level management can communicate their business value for them to senior management.

This is a major mistake. Selling professionally is complicated. Assuming that lower level management contacts who have operations, engineering, or professional service backgrounds will succinctly communicate your business value and manage all of your sales objections correctly when they go to a steering committee, decision team or short-list committee is totally wrong. They are not you. If they were you, they would be in professional sales.

Reasons Why IT Salespeople Make This Complex Selling Mistakes

When an IT salesperson's sales quota success is down, they incorrectly think that meeting with lower level contacts is better than having no prospects at all in their sales pipeline.

When the IT company does not align marketing, sales process, corporate strategy, and financial models into one defined revenue capture approach, they teach their sales team to just attempt to contact any level of entry and hope someone buys.

Hope is not a sales strategy.

Senior management prospects buy based on the value your IT product or service brings to their department or company. Lower level contacts buy based on the features, functions, or price of your product or service. Often, IT salespeople focus on the wrong value, which ends up pushing away senior management buyers and enticing lower level contacts.

Salespeople often hold onto lower level contacts hoping that if they hold on long enough, they may ultimately sell someone. That is not a sales process—it is a waiting process and most salespeople today do not have two-year sales quotas.

How should you manage a selling environment that you think is going to be complex?

In large complicated sales that involve multiple contacts with different titles that are located in different locations, learn how to penetrate the "no talk zone" of senior management and start in the "value selling zone" at the VP level and above. Contacting lower level prospects as your first entry point is a reflection of your inability to correctly communicate value to senior management.

Use prospect engagement outlines to manage lower level prospects.

When working with senior management prospects, understand why they buy and why they will not buy from you and then make them take action steps with you during your sales process so they will prove to you that they are qualified buyers.

When selling in a multi-decision environment, create marketing material and business proposals that communicate value based on how senior management sees your value...not how you see it and use it as "invisible salespeople" when you are not there.

Often large key account sales are not complex because of what the customer expects you to do—but because of the way you sell. Complex sales became complex because salespeople allow prospects to manage their sales cycle for them. So do not allow prospects to manage your sales cycle.

It's up to you!

Use the Value Forward IT Sales Method in all sized companies and sell more.

Do you make your IT sales complex?

Highlights of this section:

- IT sales are only complex when salespeople do not manage the multiple layers of a large account opportunity.

- When there are multiple decision makers and influencers in a large key account sale, you need to start at the top.

- Use prospect engagement outlines to manage lower level prospects.

Exercises:

1. Make a list of the opportunities in your pipeline that you consider complex.

2. Write down the title of the person you first spoke to regarding your offering and make an outline of the titles of individuals whom you have spoken to throughout the sales cycle. Then arrange them in order, from the top down. If you do not have a vice president or above in the list, you need to use your skills to contact the higher executive.

Chapter

7

Managing Competitors
Before They Manage You

After reading this chapter, you will learn:

- Why competitors do not always take the form of a traditional competitor

- How to keep in touch with your prospect until their buying cycle and your selling cycle intersect

It Is Not Who You Are—It Is Who You Sell Against

Since 1984, through my own IT sales and sales management career and as senior partner in the Value Forward Group (www.ValueForward.com), I have successfully competed against the largest IT players in the world. In most cases, the firms I worked for or consulted with were the new firm on the block or the small up-and-coming player taking on all newcomers or the mature IT firms in the declining stage of their company's life cycle.

If on a daily basis you are losing more business to competitors than you are winning, more than likely it is not the fault of your employer, but your IT salesmanship skills. Harsh words, but more than likely, they are true.

We all have competitors. The key is to treat your competitors like a Navy Seal would treat his enemy. In the technology sales world, it is "Hunt Now or Be Eaten Later!®" Statistically speaking, once that agreement is signed with another firm, your opportunity to close future business with that prospect is minimal.

First, let's define who your competitors are. Competitors are any firm or person who prevents you from closing your technology contract with your targeted executive within your sales quota selling timeline. Based on this definition, your competitors could be your internal operations department, your finance department, your development shop, the companies you sell against regionally, or some national player that garners trade press.

Strong words, but accurate. If you have been selling technology long enough, you will have lost major deals and commissions because your own firm did not respond expeditiously or correctly to a business opportunity.

Now I am not talking about those wild deals we all come across that don't fit our existing product or service definitions. I am talking about those clean deals where operations, finance, or your development team could not deliver the requested help or the team members you needed to close the "big" deal.

So, let's be frank. They are your competitors. Because this course is about finding, presenting, and **CLOSING** technology sales, if you ignore these internal competitors, you will not be as successful as you should be.

Let's segment each type of competitor you will meet and address how you can deal with each one. The key is **never to sell negatively**, but always to sell offensively so your competition is put in a defensive position.

Six Types of Competition in IT

Competitor 1: Your Own Company's Employees (Internal Competitors)

It is sad to say, but whether you are a five-person professional services shop or a 10,000-person major technology player, on a day-to-day basis, you have to deal with the internal competition in your company. This internal competition stands in your way of closing more technology sales and increasing your income. You cannot ignore it. It will not go away. The only way to deal with it is by identifying where the roadblocks are and putting a system in place to manage these internal impediments.

For Large Technology Sales Organizations (2,000+ employees)

Managing internal competitors is more difficult in well-established, mature selling organizations due to their entrenched corporate bureaucracy. The easiest method to deal with departments that stand in your way is to use your regional vice president or national vice president of sales as your advocate. You need to document how these departments' inability to be sales driven has affected your business sales. List examples of how the operations department did not follow up with a prospect on specific questions in a timely manner. Or how the development department failed to update the new proposal template with the technology capabilities your firm just acquired that would have helped you make the short list on an RFP. All these causes need to be documented.

The key to success with your internal competitors is to document and submit this information to your sales management team members. They have more bullets in their pistols, allowing them more diverse opportunities to try to fix these issues. It will also help to keep you as a regional rep from being shot by the vice president of operations.

Small Technology Sales Companies

If you work for a smaller technology company, you have a greater opportunity to get the internal competitors issue fixed directly. Again, document what happens and go through your sales management team to resolve these issues. If the vice president of sales is too busy or too weak, set up a meeting with the vice presidents of operations and development (if they are different people) and help educate these managers on how lost revenue opportunities hurt them just like they hurt you.

Competitor 2: Your Prospects' Existing Vendors

If you are aggressively using your SVP as a positioning tool to gain audiences with executives, and you are calling on vice presidents and above only, more than likely your prospect is either not happy with the existing vendors or your SVP is so intriguing that the company will still consider you anyway.

Remember, C-level executives do not like to waste time, so if you have an appointment, they are interested.

Competitor 3: New Technology Competitors Proposing Simultaneously

This is the real world. Nothing is easy. The key to beating competitors is to continue to be different. Focus on your **SVP** and the fact that you are specialists. When describing competitors, always refer to them as **generalists**. You can win major deals by stressing this difference. <u>Clients like working with specialists</u>, not generalists.

Competitor 4: National Technology Competitors Your Prospect Is Going to Call

One of the easiest ways to beat a large consulting company or large established technology players is using the bus metaphor. The bus metaphor relates to the common practice of large consulting or IT companies that bring senior practice managers to pitch the deal, but then deploy (bus in) inexperienced and green associates to implement or develop the technology. One of the key ways to broach this subject is to ask the decision maker if the proposal he or she has received (or will receive) lists the senior practice manager (who pitched the deal) as a full-time project manager over the project. Or is this person a shadow manager who comes and goes?

Another byproduct of dealing with big firms is that these companies are renowned for moving around their delivery teams based on changing client priorities. So, when your prospect starts expressing thoughts about using a large technology delivery team, ask if that vendor will commit in writing to having the delivery team permanently assigned (because you will).

Competitor 5: Your Prospect's Decision-Influencing Management Team

There is no question other decision-influencing managers inside your prospect's company can be your competitors. The key to dealing with this type of complex decision is to confront it before it gets out of control. If you are using the *Value Forward Sales* method correctly, you are already dealing with the decision maker directly. In bypassing lower-level decision influencers (like directors and managers), you should expect some internal politics and jealousy. But as soon as the decision maker identifies those decision influencers to you, you need to placate their egos and get them involved in the education cycle of your sale. When selling to Fortune 100 companies, the more allies and points of entry you have, the better—as long as the first entry point is a C-level executive.

Competitor 6: Build Versus Buy Option

An ever-present competitor (especially in Global 1000 sales) is the decision by technology departments to consider internal development versus a purchase. While the outsourcing and project work market space continues to grow daily, IT departments always consider internal development as an option. Internal IT departments have many reasons for considering their own project teams, but many times internal development is just empire building.

Internally developed applications and project work are generally not as feature-rich or technically robust when compared to external purchases. This stems from the revenue pressures that application and project work builders deal with that drive their organization continually to improve the product and/or project management skill sets. The higher the level of decision maker you are dealing with, the easier it will be for you to sell your services. <u>The lower in the organizational chart, the more apt the prospect is to discuss build versus buy</u>.

When faced with the discussion of build versus buy, communicate these concerns about internal development to the C-level executive, and specifically to the CFO, if you have access:

1. Internal development usually has minimal documentation.

2. Internal development usually is based on the firm's project scope and based on singular experiences whereas external development is based on many customers' input and experiences (resulting in more features).

3. By using outside technology sources, you usually have a fixed price or a budget proposal that can be contained. (Internal development usually knows no financial boundary and has scope creep.)

4. External development firms (software applications and website development) usually offer ongoing software maintenance agreements that will continually update the client's technology with new release levels and enhancements. (Internal developers many times have moved on to the next project.)

5. By using an outside vendor for development, internal departments do not have to rely on sister departments for help and support, and can bypass the traditional political environment where they have to deal with higher corporate priorities in the IT department.

Highlights of this section:

- Types of competition:

    o Your own company's employees (internal competitors)

    o Your prospect's existing vendors

    o New technology competitors proposing simultaneously

    o National technology competitors your prospect is going to call

    o Your prospect's decision-influencing management team

    o Build versus buy option

Exercises:

1. Make a list of deals you plan to close in the next 60 days. Then identify potential competitors based on the list provided in this chapter. This will help you better understand your current position as well as develop sales objection talking points.

8

Using a Technology Proposal as a Closing Tool

After reading this section, you will learn:

- How to submit a technology proposal

- How to use psychological ROI to close deals

- How to benefit from a Marketing Action Plan (MAP)

- How to use date management to increase your sales

Proposal Basics

Like business plans submitted to venture capitalists, the key to successful proposals is to submit detailed information that is consumable. Most of the time, technology proposals are all about the seller and are too technical. Cut back on the operations department's technical verbiage. Stop talking about yourself and start focusing on pain management and using your business proposals as a business success tool.

IT proposals should be invisible salespeople that sell for you when you are not there.

It's your sale.

It's your commission.

Always separate your IT proposals into two standalone binders. **Binder One** should include the business case of why your targeted buyers should buy from you and should be prepared in a wire-bound format (or something similar). **Binder Two** should include the technical case of what they will get and how it will be implemented and supported and should be prepared in a 3-ring binder.

Binder One should include:

- Your company's SVP
- Your company's history
- Brief overview of the prospect
- Business problem the prospect is trying to fix
- Description of the IT you are offering the prospect to fix the business problem
- How your IT offering will fix the business problem
- Page of commonly or frequently asked questions (FAQs) about your IT offering
- Prospect's investment to buy your offering
- List of references
- Prospect dialogue page

- Conclusion page on why the prospect should buy from you

Prospect Dialogue Page

A successful proposal tool we recommend to our clients is for them to develop a prospect dialogue page. On this page, you write down every positive comment, business improvement, or expense control effect your IT offering could have if your prospect buys your offering—**based on** what the prospect's team members say to you during the sales cycle discovery stage. Detail the person's name and title and the date and time he or she made the comment. Then in the back of Binder One, insert the specific comments made by the prospect's team members about the impact of your IT offering on their business as you were interacting with them.

Obviously, if a manager makes specific comments and says they are "confidential," you can't include them on the prospect dialogue page. But everything else is fair game.

Name this page "Your Team Members' Observations." Here is an example.

Your Team Members' Observations

During our engagement and discovery sessions with your team members, many have made specific comments about our IT offering and its impact on your business success. Here are those comments:

- Ringo Starr said on October 2 that he believes our application will decrease your labor cost by at least 2 percent.

- Paul McCartney said on October 5 that implementing our report system should accelerate management decisions.

- George Harrison said by deploying our services, department revenues should increase at least 6 percent the first year.

Why does this work?

Your prospects get to see your value three dimensionally through the eyes of their own employees. This is more credible than you saying you are great or your customer references saying it.

Make sure Binder One is readable for anyone who is non-technical (assume the CFO will be reading it), and put all the technical specifications in Binder Two. Binder One is an executive brief on why the prospect should buy. Binder Two is the "stuff" the buyer receives describing how they are serviced and what your IT offering does technically.

Binder One should NEVER be in a three-ring binder format. It can be a gum sealed binder—but never a loose leaf binder.

Why?

Because you are trying to build an executive communication document that is sequential in thought on why the prospect should buy. You want the executives to read the entire document—not pull out what they think is important.

When building a prospect IT proposal, always provide three separate options (packages/pricing) to buy. Make the targeted option you want the prospect to buy the least expensive of the three. This way if the buyer "trades down," the prospect buys the primary offering you have targeted.

Why three options?

Studies show that by giving prospects multiple price options, you make them compare you against you vs. you against a competitor. If you give them only one price or packaged IT offering choice, then you force them to seek out alternatives. Statistically, some will pick the middle option, which will increase your average sale. Always give options and make your IT buyer choose between them.

Binder Two. Insert all your technical documentation including detailed pricing, wiring specifications, rollout schedules, support timelines, training dates, interface requirements, scope expectations, hardware descriptions, and any other information the prospect needs for the purchase deployment.

My own personal bias for Binder Two is to have a three-ring binder with a custom page on the front and divided tab sections. It is more professional looking than plastic binders.

 TIP If you are selling to companies with fewer than 100 employees, always overproduce your proposal presentation to the CEO. It is not who you are, <u>it is who the CEO perceives you to be</u>.

Proposal Success Trick:

Sometimes when you are handing out a proposal in a one-to-one meeting, you as the salesperson are held captive by your audience. Often the executive will not let you go around or above him or her to other decision-making executives because of ego and control issues. So, when you develop your written Binder One proposal to be handed out in person to your direct prospect, always make additional copies for all the other decision makers and include each one's name on his or her copy's front cover. When you meet with your prospect, keep the additional copies hidden. After you have completed your proposal presentation page by page and have answered all the executive's questions, say the following:

> *Mr./Ms. Prospect, out of professional*
> *courtesy, my management team always makes*
> *extra copies of our client's proposals for the*
> *rest of your executive team. At your discretion,*
> *please pass them out.*

Then hand the executive the extra copies.

Now be careful—there is ego in the boardroom. So make sure you say, *"My management team always makes extra copies"* and *"Please pass them out at your discretion."* This way you are protected.

If your prospect is going into an executive briefing or a steering committee meeting to discuss your IT offering (and your competitors' offerings), it is a lot easier (and less work) for your contact to hand out your binder with your "Why They Should Buy" document than to re-create the materials. This way you maintain the integrity of your proposal. Instead of having a second sourced presentation manufactured by your key contact, the entire decision-making team gets to read your proposal.

Remember, IT business proposals are the invisible salespeople in the room. Without you, your proposals should be able to motivate the buyer to buy and to manage the buyer's questions as if you were there. If your proposals look like you are handing out a specification sheet with a milk order format, then maybe you should be a milkman who sells milk. If are a professional IT salesperson, then your proposal should have an integrated communication approach that makes targeted prospects want to buy from you.

Executive Technology Proposal Pitch

The entire *Value Forward Sales* method is based on a premeditated process of thinking through each step of the sales process and then packaging the action steps required. Many, many technology salespeople try to sell IT by generating proposals and sending them to prospects.

These proposals sit in those salespersons' corporate sales forecasts, as well as in their prospects' inboxes, and everyone waits for the technology sales to be approved.

Wrong!

As discussed, technology sales executives should never just send a proposal to senior level executives. Email has reduced the sales closing ratio of IT salespeople. All proposals should be delivered personally and explained in a follow-up appointment. <u>Again, the key is for you to manage the prospect, not have the prospect manage you.</u>

When your proposal is completed, call the C-level executive and say:

*Mr./Ms. X, per your request, our proposal is
ready. I would like to meet with you for 30
minutes to go through the details. It will be
quick, but we have included some unique
areas in this proposal based on your input and
your needs [LIST FIRM'S PAINS] discussed
in our presentation. I normally meet with the
CMO for 30 minutes to discuss our proposals
in person.*

Invite the executive to lunch. **Get an appointment to hand
deliver the proposal.**

If you cannot justify meeting the targeted prospect in person
because the value of your IT offering is too low, then set up a
webinar proposal instead. Create an electronic presentation
based on one page per item, and then take the prospect
through your proposal slide by slide. (Hint: You can use the
binder format for your electronic presentation.)

Never give the proposal to the prospect before the webinar
presentation—force your buyer to listen to your value step by
step.

If the prospect asks for the proposal beforehand, just say,
*"Mr./Ms. Prospect, my management team requires us to
present first before we submit a written proposal. As soon as
we are done, I will send you an electronic copy."*

If you are different, act like it; be a peer, not a vendor. Don't
you have value? Isn't your selling time important? Manage
your sales cycle, before it manages you.

How to Close More IT Deals—Psychological ROI

The strongest method for closing technology sales is through the use of psychological ROI. Early in my career, I found that value must equal price—but fear has no budget. Stronger than financial ROI, psychological ROI plays to the decision maker's personal needs and insecurities, and the business pains the company is going through.

Using psychological ROI instead of financial ROI will propel you past the average technology salesperson into the heavy hitter category. It will help you become a star IT salesperson in your company.

I have used this process with C-level executives of Fortune 100 companies and with presidents of 10-person, privately held firms. It doesn't matter how big or how small a company is, it works. Psychological ROI will help you close technology deals and increase your commissions.

Fear has no budget. Remember, many IT buyers don't know how to buy correctly—regardless of their title. So as a professional IT salesperson, you need to tell your buyers everything they need to know to make them buy.

The key to using this psychological ROI method is found at the very beginning of this book. You must be dealing with the decision maker for this process to work. That person has personal expectations, fears, and goals that drive his or her business decisions on a daily basis. Your prospect may or may not admit to these fears, but they are present. In this crazy, unstable economic environment, no one feels safe. CEOs, CFOs, CIOs, and department VPs all have to prove their value. Either they cost money or make money for the company; there is no in-between.

Direct and indirect fears (irrational at times) affect your prospects' business judgments, including:

- Being fired
- Not receiving a raise
- Not receiving a bonus
- Not being promoted
- Technology proposal costs will go over budget
- Technology proposal will affect other departments' efficiencies
- Technology recommendation will not fix the pain
- Being embarrassed in front of their subordinates
- Being embarrassed in front of their peers
- Being embarrassed in front of their boss
- Not getting additional funding from their investors
- Working too much and affecting their personal lives

Additionally, their goals are the reverse of the above list:

- To be promoted
- To be praised and noticed (remember, there's ego in the boardroom)
- To increase revenues for the company
- To spend more time with their families
- To look better than their peers in a board meeting

Identifying these fears and goals in your C-level executive contact will give you power. With power you can position your firm's technology proposal in a more positive position for market segmentation above your competitors.

So, how do we identify fears and goals of C-level executives? This process is completed through three steps:

1. Direct Statements

2. Visual Observations

3. Judgmental Observations

Direct Statements

Believe or not, many times a C-level executive will actually tell you his or her issues. You just have to listen.

Here are examples of actual comments made to me by C-level executives in Fortune 1000 companies:

> *My company is depending on this technology to help reduce our expenses and increase our stock price on Wall Street.* ***(CIO)***

> *This technology has to work or I am going to be accountable to the board.* ***(CEO)***

> *The CEO has told me that my entire department budget is at stake if we cannot reduce our overhead.* ***(Senior VP of Ops)***

> *I have had this position for six months. The last CIO was let go because he was old school and not progressive.* ***(CIO)***

Actual comments made to me by senior executives in small businesses:

> *We cannot afford to make a mistake.*
> *(CEO/Founder)*

> *Our investors expect us to increase our*
> *revenue by implementing this technology.*
> *(COO)*

So, listen, ask questions, take them to dinner, and <u>collect ammo</u>.

Visual Observations

When you meet in a senior manager's office for your 20-minute appointment, look around the office. Notice the pictures on the desk and the plaques on the walls. Who is this person? Who does he or she want you to think he or she is? What is important to him or her?

- Does he or she have a paperweight shaped like a barbell (or another symbol of power and strength)?

- Does he or she have a Harvard MBA graduation diploma on the wall?

- Does he or she have pictures on the wall of him/herself skydiving?

- Does he or she have a plaque on the wall from a technology association?

All these visuals provide information to help you determine what motivates this person, both professionally and personally.

Judgmental Observations

- Is this person in good physical shape?
- Does he or she dress well?
- Is he or she over 40 years old?
- Does he or she have leadership appeal?
- Is he or she intelligent?

Yes, these are all judgment calls you are going to have to make. <u>It's your commission at stake</u>. Reading the prospect will help you close the prospect. Salespeople of all types use these observation tools to sell to you and me. For example:

- Insurance is sold based on the **fear** of not taking care of your loved ones.
- Stock investments are sold based on **greed**.
- Jaguars are sold based on **ego** and status needs.

Based on my own personal experiences selling technology, here are some observations to use when you apply **psychological ROI**.

If a C-level executive displays any of these characteristics:

- Under 40
- Displays pictures of him/herself involved with skydiving, martial arts, scuba diving, rock climbing,

mountain bike riding, car racing, or any other adventure sport

- Wears expensive custom-made suits ($1,500 and above) or couture fashion

- Bodybuilder or extremely health conscious

- Talks fast

then he or she is driven by:

- Ego

- Adventure

- Risk taking

- Quick decisions

You should discuss how your SVP is the right choice based on these variables. You need to appeal to this executive's ego, need for adventure, and desire for risk taking.

Examples

> Mr./Ms. C-Level Executive, one reason CIOs like you invest in our technology is because they want us to provide them with the best [INSERT YOUR SVP] to increase their corporate profits.

> Mr./Ms. C-Level Executive, one reason firms like yours invest in our technology is that we give senior management executives like yourself personalized service to help maximize corporate profits through our [INSERT YOUR SVP].

Mr./Ms. C-Level Executive, one reason companies like yours invest in our technology is because they realize the Internet will not stand still for anyone. To be successful in this new economy, you must think fast and implement quickly, or else your competitors will eat your customers.

If a C-level executive displays some or all of these variables:

- Over 40
- Out of shape
- Has pictures of only his or her family in the office
- Smokes a pipe or wears traditional business attire
- Has held the same C-level position for 10 years

then he or she is driven by:

- Safety
- Security
- Patience
- Comfort

Examples

Mr./Ms. President, because our firm is a local player, we specialize in long-term, permanent relationships with our clients.

Mr./Ms. Senior Vice President of Operations, we provide a named practice manager assigned to your team so you will always have continuity of leadership

*from our firm and you will always know whom to call
if you have any questions.*

Now before you write or email me that these are vague
generalizations about C-level management types and their
assigned characterizations—**I agree**.

But the point here is to evaluate decision makers and to use
the evaluation process to appeal to their needs to close
business.

Case History – Using Collected Intel to Close the Deal

I was selling to a large international hotel company with
locations worldwide. I cold called the firm, penetrated the C-
suite and met the CIO and the CFO for my 20-minute
meeting. During the conversation, the CIO said (in front of
the CFO) that he was new and was an action type of guy,
unlike the previous CIO, who had been terminated.

He stated very directly that he would not fail; he was a
"runner" not a "walker" when it came to making smart
business decisions.

This personal admission by the CIO during my 20-minute
meeting became my psychological ROI driver during my
proposal closing. When final negotiations slowed down, I
mentioned in a telephone call to the CIO that he was not like
his predecessor and that his company must be very pleased he
was making fast business decisions to implement success
changes. He agreed—and he signed my contract a week later.

Price Is Not Always Relevant

When selling technology and professional services to C-level executives, price usually comes out on surveys as being the fifth or sixth most important ingredient on the list.

Do I believe it?

Yes, with a caveat.

Price is never an issue if you can separate yourself from everyone else by presenting your SVP.

Price is _always_ an issue if you look like and sound like everyone else.

Price must equal value, or it's too much money. When someone tells you your IT offering is too high, then it means you have incorrectly described your business value.

Case History – Pricing

A few years ago, I was selling a packaged offering for software, services, and consulting to a Fortune 500 entertainment company headquartered in the United States. My price for this package for the first year was $900,000.00. The prospect had short-listed my firm, along with one of my strongest competitors, and had invited us both in to discuss our proposals. My competitor was also a Fortune 500 company, and his first-year price came in at $350,000.00.

When I met with the C-level management team, the members aggressively pressured me to explain why my price was $550,000.00 more than this well-known and established technology player.

I laid out my elevator pitch slowly and directly.

1. I explained my SVP again.

2. I reconfirmed that we were specialists, **not** generalists.

3. I focused on the pains they had described in our executive briefing meeting.

4. I explained again how my SVP would fix their pains and increase profits.

5. I focused on how selecting the wrong vendor because of price would affect their stated project outcome. Additionally, I said short-term savings could create a tidal wave of expense on the back end when they tried to fix the mistake of selecting the wrong vendor.

Then, as a final shot across the table, I said, *to be honest, I would be nervous if you are getting a low-ball price. What do you think they are leaving out?*

Yes, I won the deal even though we were hundreds of thousands of dollars above our nearest competitor. Why? Because I created a value proposition the prospect could not ignore. Even though there was a large difference between the price points, I forced the prospect to face reality. When the prospect approached vendor number two, all this IT company talked about was the great price it offered.

MAP Management

One of the most effective tools for personal sales time management is called a **MAP**. Everyone who works for me knows what this tool is. Once a month, we sit down and evaluate each prospect in the sales pipeline forecasted to close that month, and together we develop a monthly MAP. MAP stands for a **Marketing Action Plan**, and it is a detailed list of dates and action steps required to close business that month. MAPS are tools that help technology salespeople close business.

So, if you are looking to close more technology sales, on the first of every month, lay out a MAP, account by account.

A **MAP** includes:

- Prospect's name
- Contact person's name
- Type of proposal (design, development, software, etc.)
- Short-term dollar opportunity value (first 12 months)
- Long-term dollar opportunity value (1-5 years)
- Sales steps completed so far and on what dates
- Next sales steps to be completed and on what dates
- Help from senior management and operations needed to complete the sale
- What the competitive environment is like
- Open issues that need to be managed

By laying out in detail every month the expected IT sales opportunities you expect to close, you will find your closing ratio will go up. Again, we are focusing on premeditated sales steps to close in that month specifically. Remember, you want the prospect to take transactional action steps with you in tandem to reconfirm over and over again that they are qualified and are in an active buying cycle ... and not wasting your time.

An IT salesperson's income is totally connected to the correct use of his or her productive time. More than time management—it is Strategic Productivity™. Strategic Productivity is linking your actions to your personal and professional objectives so that both are met. To earn more and work less, you need to work smarter, focused on working with prospects who are qualified and who take action steps with you in tandem within the time frame you need to be successful. Becoming a successful IT salesperson, becoming a rich IT salesperson, requires you to be premeditated in your sales cycle within time barriers. Selling $3 million in technology over three years has a different effect on your income and your career than selling $3 million in 12 months.

By using the MAP process (see example on the following pages), you will identify for yourself (and your sales management) the issues that are barriers to closing the sale and what is needed to close the business this month.

Additionally, in the Appendix, I have provided a detailed Account Sales Planning Worksheet. By focusing on these steps, you will walk to the close and become a successful, premeditated technology salesperson.

Success Note: When forecasting IT sales on a monthly basis, if by the first of the month your target prospect (the decision maker and contract signer) has not received your final proposal, do not forecast that deal to be closed in that month. IT deals, both large and small, take time to process through the targeted prospect's organizational departments and thought process. Legal departments, purchasing managers, decision influencers, decision makers' vacations, and just slow bureaucracy inhibit contract signings. There are only 20 business days a month, not counting vacations and holidays, so statistically, getting a signed agreement within one month of a proposal's receipt is unusual.

Date Management

Another key ingredient in closing technology sales faster is the process of using a **Date Management Plan** (see example on the following pages) as a success tool. On a daily basis, many technology salespeople sell their management on the accuracy of their sales forecasts and the expected monthly revenues tied to it. I am surprised how often experienced technology salespeople forecast an opportunity about to be closed without dates attached to the sales closing steps.

In my firm, if all sales steps cannot be completed by the 15th of the month, we do not forecast that deal for that month, regardless if the C-level executive says he or she is making the decision by the 30th.

In technology deals, <u>time is a competitor.</u>

So, to sell more, attach a forecasted date on your date management form to each sales step after you talk with the prospect the first time. It will force you to work off the dates in a planned process, and you will close more business on time.

Example

Marketing Action Plan (MAP)

Month_____
Date Prepared_____
Account Manager_____

Client Name_____
Client Contact _____
Proposal Type _____
Proposal Value _____

Sales Steps Completed So Far

Completed	Step	Date Completed or To Be Completed
Yes/No	Telephone Call	_____
Yes/No	1st Appointment	_____
Yes/No	2nd Appointment	_____
Yes/No	Product/Service Presentation	_____
Yes/No	Proposal Completed	_____
Yes/No	Proposal Submitted	_____
Yes/No	Proposal Reviewed in Person	_____
Yes/No	Proposal Negotiation	_____
Yes/No	Objections Reviewed	_____
Yes/No	Legal Reviews Contract	_____
Yes/No	Contract Signed	_____

Other steps needed/Help required: _____
_____

Competitors involved: _____
_____

Open issues: _____
_____

Why will they buy? _____
_____

Why will they *not* buy? _____
_____

How are we creating value they believe? _____
_____

How will our offering increase the buyer's income, decrease expenses, or manage business risks? _____
_____

What is the name and title of the buyer?_____
_____

Date contract should be in-house: _____
_____

Example

Date Management Plan

Month_____
Date Prepared_____
Account Manager_____

Prospect Name _____
Prospect Company _____

Proposal Type _____
Proposal Value _____

Sales Steps

Completed	Step	Date Completed or To Be Completed
Yes/No	Telephone Call	_____
Yes/No	1st Appointment	_____
Yes/No	2nd Appointment	_____
Yes/No	Product/Service Presentation	_____
Yes/No	Proposal Completed	_____
Yes/No	Proposal Submitted	_____
Yes/No	Proposal Reviewed in Person	_____
Yes/No	Proposal Negotiation	_____
Yes/No	Objections Reviewed	_____
Yes/No	Legal Reviews Contract	_____
Yes/No	Contract Signed	_____

Other Steps Needed/Help Required: _____
_____
_____

Vendor Roadblocks: _____
_____
_____

Competitors Involved: _____
_____

Competitive Roadblocks: _____
_____

Open Issues: _____
_____
_____

Highlights of this section:

- Direct and indirect fears (irrational at times) affect your prospects' business judgments.

- Price must equal value, or your offering is too much money.

- Time is a competitor.

Exercises:

1. Next time you are in an executive's office, observe the surroundings and make a mental note. Try to determine quickly whether the executive is a risk taker or a conservative decision maker.

2. Sit down and evaluate each prospect in your sales pipeline forecasted to close this month. Develop a monthly MAP.

Chapter

9

Conclusion

B y now you have learned the successful tactics, best practices, strategic positioning, and communication vernacular to be a more successful technology salesperson. While reading this book, you potentially may have run across concepts and ideas that were new or challenging to your established sales training experiences and sales process approaches. At the Value Forward Group, we have trained tens of thousands of IT salespeople from small, privately held IT companies to Global 50 players. These are proven methods that work. But there is one business success attribute we can't teach you that can become a roadblock for you to be the top IT salesperson in your company.

Ambition

Ambition is not a packaged, teachable skill set—either you have it or you don't. Selling is a profession. It is a high-paying profession. It is sometimes easy as an IT salesperson to hang on to your salary, bury your sales opportunities into a sales forecast, and keep postponing your deals into perpetuity without your management team holding you accountable. But if you are not selling your assigned sales quotas, and you are living off your high IT base salary—then you are not a truly professional salesperson.

Maybe you should look for another job.

Using our methods without ambition will limit your success.

But if you want to be wildly successful and want to make more money that you ever thought possible, couple your ambition with our methods and you will be unstoppable.

So, to be great, you must work hard, plan your actions, think about what you are going to say, and Hunt Now ... or Be Eaten Later!®

To help you implement the *Value Forward Sales* method, I have also included a 60-day action plan in Appendix A. Follow through on this plan, and you should see a dramatic increase in your technology sales commissions almost immediately.

Thanks for your support, and please let me know about your technology sales successes and how my firm can help you accelerate your revenue capture.

Hunt Now or Be Eaten Later!®

Paul DiModica
Value Forward Group
pdimodica@valueforward.com
770.632.7647

Appendix A
60-Day Value Forward
Action Plan

The following plan is a strategic and tactical deployment blueprint to help you increase your technology sales commissions and to propel your revenue upward. This is an *actual* technology sales development plan I have used to help launch a technology company. You may use all of it or any segment you deem appropriate to help you increase your technology sales. Depending on your budget and your personal goals, this blueprint can be accelerated or elongated in time, based on your needs. This plan will produce customer leads, sales opportunities, and quick market identification for you and your business in your local market space.

Week One

- Start creating your Sales Value Proposition (SVP).

- Go to your top 10 prospects' websites in each of the verticals your firm sells to and print out 10 pages from each website.

- Circle the common words and messages expressed on these web pages.

- Start writing down multiple SVP examples. Be creative. Seek to produce at least 20 prototypes for review.

- Start planning your executive seminar series. Shoot for your first date to be eight weeks from today. Pick a topic.

- Select five SVP examples from your master list of 20. Test them out on your coworkers. Select one that best positions your company as being different.

- Start designing your marketing materials to match your new SVP.

- Start scripting your new SVP's telemarketing script.

- Start designing a postcard with your SVP.

Week Two

- Update your website's home page with your SVP.

- Finish your postcard design. Send it to the printer.

- Finish your marketing collateral design. Send it to the printer.

- Select the venue for your seminar series. Contact the venue and reserve four dates over the next four months.

- Try out your new SVP telemarketing script on your work associates. Develop your objection management script to accompany the telemarketing script.

- Select a business book to send to C-level executives. Review the book to confirm there is no objectionable material inside.

- Create a list of 50 companies/executives to which you want to send the book.

- Meet with associated strategic partners and ask them to speak at one of your four upcoming seminars.

Week Three

- Inspect the seminar's location to confirm the space. Shoot for a facility that can hold 150 people comfortably. Sign the agreement.

- Start telemarketing your new SVP to C-level executives. Shoot for 50 new cold calls a day. (Stockbrokers do 100 a day.) Set up appointments.

- Buy your 50 books.

- Design your seminar invitation with an RSVP (like a wedding invitation) for your upcoming seminars (include all four dates), and send it to the printer.

- Attend one evening networking function.

Week Four

- Pick up your completed marketing materials postcards, and seminar invitations.

- Pick up your completed postcards.

- Pick up your completed seminar invitations.

- Mail seminar invitations to 2,000 prospects, existing and past clients, and the press.

- Mail 50 books to C-level prospects.

- Continue cold calling every day. Set up appointments.

- Submit seminar outline to partner speakers.

- Create **"Executive Sponsorship"** overview to sell sponsorships for your executive seminars. Sell them at $12,000.00 for each seminar or $40,000.00 for all four.

Week Five

- Keep cold calling. Set up appointments.

- Contact the 50 C-level executives who received the book, and set up appointments.

- Mail 1,000 postcards to C-level executives.

- Cold call partners to sell seminar sponsorships.

- Place an advertisement in the business section of your local Sunday paper about the upcoming seminar.

- Request 20 questions from each seminar speaker for review.

- Contact editors of local papers to have lunch and talk about your business seminar series.

- Attend one networking function. Invite all C-level contacts you meet to your seminar.

Week Six

- Keep cold calling. Set up appointments.

- Send out another 2,000 invitations to the same C-level executives. This will be their second invitation.

- Attend two networking functions.

Week Seven

- Keep cold calling. Set up appointments.

- Meet with your seminar presenters to go through the format.

- Send out RSVP confirmations to seminar attendees.

- Mail out 2,000 new postcards to C-level executives.

- Attend two networking functions.

Week Eight

- Keep cold calling. Set up appointments.

- Attend one networking function.

- Hold your seminar.

- Mail out 50 more books to new C-level executive prospects.

- After the first seminar, mail out 2,000 invitations to the next seminar.

- Meet with new speakers for the second seminar.

- Meet with local press for lunch. Pitch a story.

Appendix B
Industry Magazines, Books, and Associations

Magazines

CFO
www.cfo.com

Chief Executive Magazine
www.chiefexecutive.com

Information Week
www.informationweek.com

Books

Advanced Rhinocerology (The Rhino Books) by Scott Robert Alexander

Associations

American Electronics Association
www.aeanet.org

Association of Internet Professionals
www.internetprofessionals.org

Business and Technology Alliance (TAG)
www.tagonline.org

Business Marketing Association
www.marketing.org

Independent Computer Consultants Association
www. icca.org

TechServe Alliance (formerly the National Association of
Computer Consultant Businesses)
www.techservealliance.org

National Association of Women Business Owners
www.nawbo.org

The Indus Entrepreneurs
www.tie.org

Appendix C
Lead Generation and
Management

Database Contact Lists

Data.com .... www.data.com

Dun & Bradstreet .... www.dnb.com

Hoover's Online .... www.hoovers.com

OneSource .... www.onesource.com

Database Contact Management

NetSuite .... www.netsuite.com

Oracle .... www.oracle.com

SalesForce.com .... www.salesforce.com

SalesLogix .... www.saleslogix.com

SAP .... www.sap.com

Appendix D
Example Forms

First Appointment Talking Points Form

Date Prepared_____
Account Manager_____

Prospect's Name_____

Appointment Contacts

Name_____Title_____
Name_____Title_____
Name_____Title_____

Business Type_____
Public/Private_____ Number of Employees_____
Business URL_____
Industry Business Pains_____
Industry Terminology_____
Our **Sales Value Proposition** to communicate_____
_____

Our Associates' Talking Points:
Associate's Name_____
Talking Points He/She Should Cover_____

Associate's Name_____
Talking Points He/She Should Cover_____

Subject Area to Avoid_____
Meeting Goal_____
Goal Time Period_____
Potential Purchase_____
Value of Opportunity Over One Year_____
Additional Comments_____

Three Box Monty

Executive Presentation Format
Length: 1 - 1½ hours

Team Prep	Minutes
• Presenter group arrives at least 30 minutes early. Meets in parking lot.	30

Presentation

		Minutes
1.	Presenter introductions/business cards are handed out.	**2.5**
2.	Introduce attendees.	**2.5**
3.	Lead presenter (salesperson) confirms the amount of time available for the presentation.	--
4.	Lead presenter reconfirms the business pains expressed by the management contact coupled with industry pains.	**5**
5.	Lead presenter launches into slide presentation (eight slides or fewer) giving company history, client list, and SVP.	**10**
6.	Three Box Monty presentation (depending on if you have an IT product or a specialized service to explain).	**15-30**
7.	Optional step: Service or product presenter launches into a screen shot or reports presentation of what is being sold. If not, move on to Step 8.	**15-30**
8.	Executive Briefing Close	**10**
	Client Q&A. Wrap-up. Ask transactional questions of the senior executive to confirm he/she is still qualified.	

Executive Presentation Talking Points

Lead Presenter's Name (salesperson):_____

Client's name_____

Client's URL_____

Client's Address/Briefing Location_____

Briefing Date_____Briefing Time_____

Time Allocated to Briefing by Client_____

Meeting Lead Attendee:

Name_____ Title_____Telephone_____

Meeting Attendees:

Name_____ Title_____Telephone_____

Name_____ Title_____Telephone_____

Name_____ Title_____Telephone_____

Client's Pain Issues_____

Product or Service To Be Presented_____

Presenter's Name_____

Title_____

Responsible for Presentation Slide (List slide number/subject)_____

Presenter's Name_____

Title_____

Responsible for Presentation Slide (List slide number/subject)_____

Presenter's Name_____

Title_____

Responsible for Presentation Slide (List slide number/subject)_____

Presenter's Name_____

Title_____

Responsible for Slide/Whiteboard Presentation (List slide number/subject)_____

Goal of Presentation_____
_____

What does the prospect want to see/hear at the meeting?_____

Current product/service being used by the prospect_____

_____

Current business pain with existing product or service_____

_____

What do we want to sell them?_____

What is the dollar value for the first year?_____

What is the dollar value of this client over the next three years?_____

Do they have a budget?　　　　　_____Yes　　_____No

If yes, how much?_____

When do they want this product or service?_____

Why will they buy from us?_____

Why will we lose this deal?_____

Which contact is signing the purchase order/contract?_____

Which contact(s) is (are) making the decision?_____

Is there a consultant involved?　　　　_____Yes　　_____No
　　　　If yes, what is the consultant's name?_____
　　　　Consultant's company name_____
　　　　Consultant's telephone_____
　　　　Is the consultant: For us_____ Against us_____ Neutral_____

What are the prospect's business consequences if they do
not buy from us?_____

_____

What does the selling team need to do to close this business?_____

_____

Are there any unusual marketing expenses needed to close this business?_____

_____

Next Action Steps_____

Marketing Action Plan (MAP)

Month_____
Date Prepared_____
Account Manager_____

Client Name_____
Client Contact _____
Proposal Type_____
Proposal Value _____

Sales Steps Completed So Far

Completed	Step	Date Completed or To Be Completed
Yes/No	Telephone Call	_____
Yes/No	1st Appointment	_____
Yes/No	2nd Appointment	_____
Yes/No	Product/Service Presentation	_____
Yes/No	Proposal Completed	_____
Yes/No	Proposal Submitted	_____
Yes/No	Proposal Reviewed in Person	_____
Yes/No	Proposal Negotiation	_____
Yes/No	Objections Reviewed	_____
Yes/No	Legal Reviews Contract	_____
Yes/No	Contract Signed	_____

Other steps needed/Help required: _____
_____

Competitors involved: _____
_____

Open issues: _____
_____

Why will they buy? _____
_____

Why will they *not* buy? _____
_____

How are we creating value they believe? _____
_____

How will our offering increase the buyer's income, decrease expenses, or manage business risks? _____
_____

What is the name and title of the buyer?_____
_____

Date contract should be in-house: _____
_____

Account Sales Planning Worksheet

Date Prepared_____

Account Manager Assigned_____

Account Name_____

Account Location_____

Account Telephone_____

Key Contacts

Name_____Title_____

Name_____Title_____

Name_____Title_____

Name_____Title_____

Name_____Title_____

Corporate Organization Overview

Known Divisions

_____

_____

_____

_____

_____

_____

_____

1. Is there an installed vendor?
   Yes   No

   If yes, who?_____

2. Is there a corporate-wide recommended vendor?
   Yes   No

   If yes, who?_____

3. How long has this company been the recommended vendor?
   _____

4. Have we sold any of this prospect's other operating divisions?
   Yes   No

   If yes, which one(s)?_____

   If yes, can we leverage these relationships?_____

   How?_____

   _____

   _____

5. How is this decision being made? (Mark all that apply)

   o   Steering Committee

   o   Short List

   o   Consultant

   o   RFP

   o   RFI

   o   Other

6. What other divisions are using this recommended vendor?_____

    _____

    _____

7. Current business pain with existing product or service or vendor?___

    _____

    _____

8. What do we want to sell to the prospect?_____

    _____

    _____

9. What is the business dollar value the first year?_____

    _____

10. What is the business dollar value potential of the prospect over the next three years?_____

    _____

11. Does the prospect have a stated budget?
    Yes   No

    If yes, how much?_____

12. When does the prospect want this product or service installed?_____

    _____

13. When does the prospect want to be operational?_____

14. Why will the prospect buy from us?_____

    _____

    _____

15. Why will we lose this deal?_____

    _____

    _____

16. How will we create value the prospect will believe?_____

    _____

    _____

17. Which contact(s) is/are making the decision?_____

_____

18. Is a consultant involved?
Yes   No

If yes, provide the consultant's name, company, and telephone number.

_____

_____

Is the consultant:
for us?_____ against us?_____ neutral?_____

19. What are the prospect's business consequences if the prospect does not buy from us?_____

_____

20. What does the selling team need to do to close this business?_____

_____

21. Do we need to get operations, engineering, finance, or other departments involved in helping us sell this deal? If yes, which departments?_____

_____

_____

22. Are there unusual marketing expenses needed to close this business?

_____

_____

_____

Next Action Steps

23. Do we have a key account organizational chart of the decision team?
Yes   No

24. Who will be signing the contract (name and title)_____

_____

25. Will the contract have to go to purchasing?
Yes   No

Key Contract Signer Name & Title_____
_____
Key Contract Signer Approach Strategies_____
_____
_____
_____

Contract Decision Maker Name & Title_____
_____
Contract Decision Maker Approach Strategies_____
_____
_____
_____

Contract Decision Maker Name & Title_____
_____

Contract Decision Maker Approach Strategies_____
_____
_____
_____

Contract Decision Maker Name & Title_____
_____

Contract Decision Maker Approach Strategies_____
_____
_____
_____

Contract Decision Maker Name & Title_____
_____

Contract Decision Maker Approach Strategies_____
_____
_____
_____

Contract Decision Maker's Political Environment_____

_____
_____
_____
_____

Return on Investment - R.O.I. Expectations by Decision Makers_____

_____
_____
_____
_____

Return on Investment - ROI Calculation Method for This Sale_____

_____
_____
_____
_____

Are there any relationships to the prospect within our existing customer base?
Yes   No

If yes, with whom?_____

_____
_____

Other Important Information About This Sale_____

_____
_____
_____
_____

Index

About Paul DiModica

Paul DiModica is the Founder and CEO of the Value Forward Group (www.valueforward.com), a High Tech Business Growth Acceleration firm that integrates marketing, financial management, organizational development design, strategy, operations and sales process into one outbound revenue capture program. The Value Forward Group is a worldwide management consortium of management advisors made up of former CEOs, VPs of Sales, VPs of Operation, VPs of Strategy and VPs of Marketing of both public and private companies.

Value Forward works with start-ups, investor funded players, family-run businesses and public companies.

Prior to founding the Value Forward Group in 2001, Paul also founded, e4Speed, a technology managed services, staffing and software project development firm with 45+ employees now owned by a Fortune 1000 company. In 1996, Paul also launched iInform a hospitality automation firm that rented (SaaS) Intelligence (BI) information software to restaurant chains using a touch internet screen browser accessed through the POS system.

Prior to launching his own companies, Paul spent eighteen years working with CEOs in business start-ups, Inc. 500 firms and Fortune 1000 companies. He has held the position of Vice President of Sales and Marketing for Encore Systems, Vice President of Sales for CLS, Senior Vice President of Sales and Marketing at Impressa, Vice President of Operations for Tri-State Systems and Vice President

Worldwide of Strategic Development for Renaissance
Worldwide (a $900 million public company), reporting
directly to the CEO and the Board of Directors. At
Renaissance, Paul evaluated the divisional presidents'
performances for the board of directors.

Paul has been featured or interviewed by the *New York
Times, Investors Daily, Fox News, Selling Power Magazine,
Sales and Marketing Magazine, CIO Magazine, CFO
Magazine, Entrepreneur Magazine, Training Magazine,
Marketing Magazine, Transport Times, Computer World
Magazine, Entrepreneur Radio, Chicago Tribune, The
Cleveland Sunday Paper, Kansas City Small Business
Monthly, The Manager's Intelligence Report, Agent's Sales
Journal, Executive Travel Magazine, Wisconsin Professional
Journal, Time Compression Technologies Magazine,
Minorities and Women Magazine, Broker Agent News, World
Fence News, Affluent Magazine, Value Added Partners, The
Merchant Magazine, Pennsylvania Business Central
Magazine*, and many others.

Weekly IT Business Success Newsletter

HighTechSuccess

HighTechSuccess is designed for IT corporate executives in growth directed firms. It provides tips on sales, strategy and marketing techniques to increase your business success.

Sign up today!
www.HighTechSuccess.com

High Tech CEO & Team Services

High Tech 360° Business Success Assessment and Recommendations Program

The Value Forward High Tech 360° Business Model Success and Recommendations Program is a compressive detailed program designed to help companies integrate financial management, marketing, strategy, operations and sales into one outbound revenue capture program. Through our program, we evaluate your business from your prospect's point of view, then from the management team's point of view, and then recommend specific detailed action steps to close the gap between how you see yourself and how prospects see you. Once these recommendations are made, we then work with you and you team in tandem to implement our suggestions.

Value Forward Guided Progress Success (GPS) System

The Value Forward GPS System is a 12-month planned business success program designed to give growth directed clients a step-by-step architectural blueprint to improve their firm's performance.

Using our three sequential stages of analyzing, strategizing and monetizing, we work with senior executives to help build a replicable and scalable revenue capture program based on their goals, their company's core competencies, and industry best practices. A detailed written list of action steps is provided and through a collaborative process, we work with the management team in tandem to execute changes to the business design and operational framework to maximize their corporate success.

IT Team Strategy, Marketing and Sales Training Success Workshops and Keynotes

At the Value Forward Group, we offer a broad range of programs and services designed to help sales and marketing teams grow their business revenue and build scalable and replicable revenue capture programs. Our sales training and strategy programs are designed to help you and your team "become a peer in the boardroom, instead of a vendor waiting in the hallway®." Through specific Value Forward tactical techniques and methods, we teach you how to put your business value in front of you so your prospects see you as strategic advisor and take action steps to buy.

**Call us today at (770) 632-7647
or visit www.ValueForward.com**

We can custom-fit our programs based on your business needs and budgets.

Get $97.00 FREE Value Forward Sales Bonus
"How to Get a Better Sales Job or Promotion"

*Email is required in order to notify you about your shipment. (Please print)

Name_____

Title_____

Business Name_____

Address_____

City_____State_____Zip_____

Email_____

Phone_____Fax_____

Providing this information constitutes your permission for Paul DiModica to contact you regarding related Value Forward information via email and fax.

Fax this completed page to 877-238-1828

We do not ship outside of the United States for free. If you are outside the United States, have bought this book, and are interested in receiving this bonus content for FREE—please contact us for shipping costs.

CPSIA information can be obtained at www.ICGtesting.com
Printed in the USA
BVOW02s2036071113

335744BV00005B/139/P